Praise For

This book is a profound exploration of emotional intelligence, blending years of professional insight with deeply personal experiences. Dr. Gregory Stewart masterfully navigates the complexities of human emotion and thought, offering readers a clear framework to unlock their emotional resilience and strength. I³ empowers individuals to confront and transform their emotional challenges, leading to personal growth and a deeper understanding of their identity, value, and worth. This book is not only an invaluable resource for leaders, counselors, and coaches but also for anyone seeking personal transformation through the integration of faith, self-awareness, and emotional health.

Angie Richey, Ph.D., LMFT
President, Life Pacific University

I³: Unlock the Inner Strength Behind Your Negative Emotions is an invaluable resource that transforms complex psychological concepts into accessible, actionable guidance. By revealing the hidden potential of our negative emotions, this book empowers readers to turn their struggles into catalysts for personal growth and resilience.

Tom Alexander, Ph.D., L.P.C.
Assistant Program Director, Ph.D. in Counseling and Psychological Studies & Assistant Professor
Regent University, College of Health and Behavioral Sciences

Greg is well positioned both by education and experience to blend the physiological and the spiritual. Greg blends the psychological and the spiritual brilliantly. A one/two punch.

Gordon Daam
Pastor and Mentor to Greg

Dr. Stewart's I^3 succinctly and poignantly delineates the purpose of powerful emotions and how to harness the energy created to accomplish meaningful goals without sacrificing the core of who one is. Dr. Stewart breathes fresh insight that illuminates the soul's deepest needs and how to meet those needs in more adaptive and healthier ways. Dr. Stewart's illustrations are impactful yet relatable in ways that other authors seem to miss.

Debby Morris, LPC-A

I^3 Unlocking the Inner Strength Behind Your Negative Emotions is a transformative guide based on scholarship, experience, and the author's own authentic journey. The honesty in these pages and the powerful concepts presented will help many work through their negative emotions and discover their potential as catalysts for personal growth. I highly recommend I^3 and look forward to living and leading what I have learned from Dr. Greg Stewart.

Rev. Dr. Brian D. Bennett
Lead Pastor, Pathway Church, Vero Beach, FL

I³ Information Interpretation Intensity

C 2024 Greg Stewart

All rights reserved. No part of this publication may be reproduced, distributed, or transmitted in any form or by any means, including photocopying, recording, or other electronic or mechanical methods, without the prior written permission of the publisher, except in the case of brief quotations embodied in critical reviews and certain other noncommercial uses permitted by copyright law. For permission requests, write to the publisher, addressed "Attention: Permissions Coordinator:" at the address below:

Greg Stewart

Rockwall, TX

Gregstewart@becomingmore.com

Ordering Information:

Special discounts are available on quantity purchases by corporations, associations, educational institutions, and others. For details, contact Greg Stewart above.

Printed in the United States of America

First Edition

Softcover ISBN 978-1-66641-059-4

Ebook ISBN 978-1-66641-060-0

LCCN: 2024944742

Publisher

Winsome Entertainment Group LLC

Murray, UT

By weaving together candid stories, actionable guidance, and spiritual insights, Unlock the Inner Strength Behind Your Negative Emotions *reframes emotional challenges as stepping stones to personal growth, empowering readers to harness their feelings for greater resilience and a life of authenticity.*

Jessica Guilfoyle, Ph.D., LMFT
Program Director, Ph.D. in Counseling and Psychological Studies, Regent University

This book powerfully illustrates the author's commitment to helping others through his shared experiences and reflections on personal growth. It's a relatable and meaningful legacy for anyone aiming to unlock their inner strength and live authentically. As a Licensed Professional Counselor, I read a lot of self-help literature, but I rarely come across gems that I wholeheartedly recommend to my clients. This book is an exceptional resource for those seeking to understand the deeper aspects of their emotional struggles and learn how to navigate them effectively. I would recommend this book to every client!"

Alyssa Pena, M.S., LPC

This book takes readers on a profound journey of self-discovery, encouraging them to confront their negative emotions and transform them into sources of strength.

Matthew Carlson, LPC, LMHC

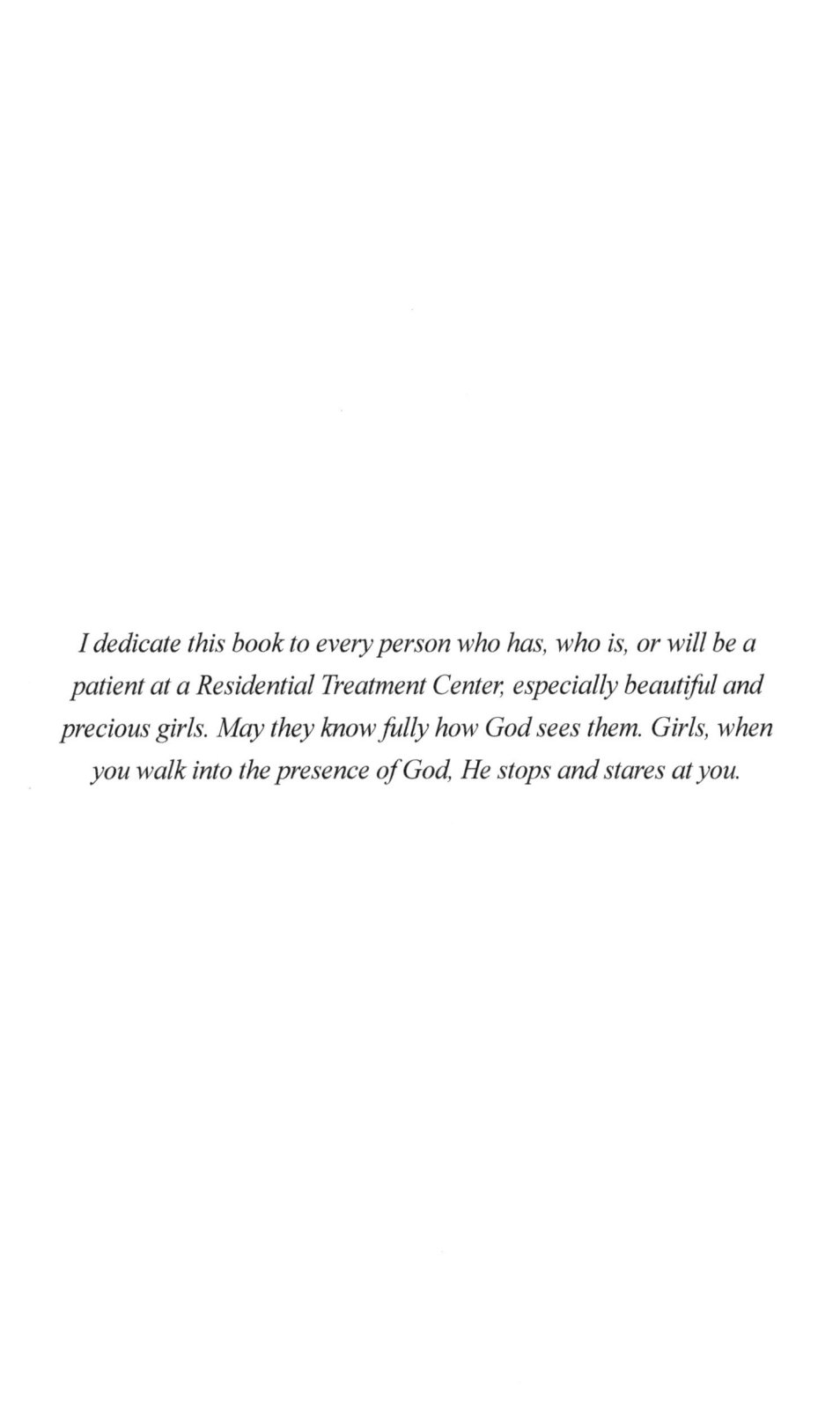

I dedicate this book to every person who has, who is, or will be a patient at a Residential Treatment Center, especially beautiful and precious girls. May they know fully how God sees them. Girls, when you walk into the presence of God, He stops and stares at you.

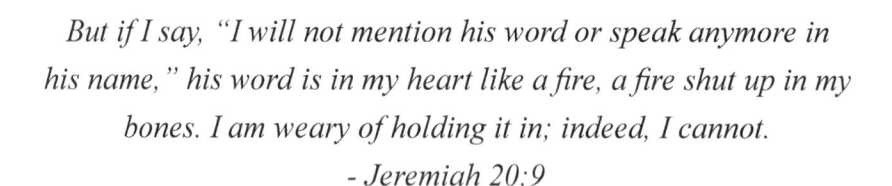

But if I say, "I will not mention his word or speak anymore in his name," his word is in my heart like a fire, a fire shut up in my bones. I am weary of holding it in; indeed, I cannot.
- Jeremiah 20:9

Table of Contents

Foreword 1

Preface 7

Acknowledgements 8

Introduction 9

Chapter 1: The Stories We Tell Ourselves 12

Chapter 2: The Blind Can't See 37

Chapter 3: Our Emotional Storms 70

Chapter 4: The Matrix of Insecurity 87

Chapter 5: Identity, Value, & Worth 99

Chapter 6: That Which Threatens Me 125

Chapter 7: The Gift of Trauma 145

Chapter 8: I^3 – Information, Interpretation, Intensity 163

Foreword

What struck me right away about this book was the proposal that negative emotions are not bad. Take one of the negative emotions, like fear. Yes, that is a negative emotion, and who wants to experience fear? But fear is something God created and allowed us to have to protect our lives, protect our safety or security, or cause us to react to protect those around us. So even though fear is a negative emotion, we don't want to avoid it, we want to use it to help us, so on the contrary, it's positive. I thought the same thing concerning anger. As believers, we think we're not supposed to get angry, but there is a place for it. We should be angry at sin, at our own behavior sometimes, which in the end increases our security and safety.

The expression of our emotions can be a great thing, that is why I love the Book of Psalms. If King David lived today, I believe he'd love social media and have thousands of followers, because, as an artiste, a poet and musician, his feelings are just out there, and he's expressing his emotions all the time. The key difference, however, between King David and our current culture is he didn't wallow in it. He doesn't stay there, and eventually he goes back to the Lord. David recognizes his own heart is the problem, and he recognizes God is sovereign. David rehearses and celebrates God's promises, God's providence, God's protection, and God's provision that never changes.

We are the ones who need to change, and if we're going to make real change *inside us*, it must come from *outside us*. because we are finite. We're limited, so we need outside objective truth and power to guide us and equip us to become better. In each situation, we need to realize we don't have enough information. We might be wrong or incorrect, because we have sinful hearts, deceitful hearts the Scripture says, and sin itself has blinded us, whether it be our own sin or the sin from the fallen world in which we live.

The great paradox of all of this is when Greg states that everything we do is trying to achieve an emotional goal. The emotional goal is always good, but we always struggle using irrational, unhealthy, unwise, and wrong pathways to achieve these emotional goals. That is our sin. It all comes down to the heart. The heart's desire is to be free to use any pathway it wants to achieve very good and emotional goals, like love and empathy, but many in our culture want complete freedom to choose any behavior they desire to achieve those emotions. It is what we call *deconstructionism*, or the shift from concrete truths to emphasizing the fluidity of language and meaning. Our culture is trying to move as far away from absolute truth as possible, to not be bound by anything proposing itself to be right, which makes certain things wrong. However, as Greg points out throughout his book, no one can escape the universal guidelines of rational, healthy, wise, and right.

In conversations with Greg, I picked up that he refers to himself as a *theological* counselor, instead of a Christian or Biblical counselor. He does this because the end goal for all of us is to align ourselves with the character of God. Defining himself as a Christian counselor places the focus on how he identifies himself as a follower of Christ; and defining himself as a Biblical counselor means his main verbiage in counseling comes from the Scriptures. Neither of these are wrong, but he believes it trips people into a hole that distracts them from the true essence of what he is trying to do, i.e., help people live the most rational, healthy, wise, and right lives, which points right to the very character and nature of God. The point of what Greg is saying is that negative emotions make us pay attention to something that isn't right. These emotions are not to be avoided but are to be first assessed and evaluated to see if they are rational, healthy, wise, and right, and then used to correct things in ourselves and things around us to become more aligned with the character of God.

Many in our culture automatically validate their emotions and are offended at the suggestion their emotions may need to change. What they need to understand is that what they are feeling is true, but that doesn't automatically mean those emotions are based in truth. This interchange has been the basis of the human experience since the beginning. Satan want people to feel the emotion of loss, which opens the door for him to suggest that the loss is bad and then suggests his ways to fill that loss. By doing this, the focus shifts from right behaviors that produce right emotions to negative emotions being the enemy, which grants the permission to take any pathway to "fix" the negative emotions. That is essentially what deconstructionism is, the shifting from black-and-white truths to a more nebulous and gray evaluation of one's own emotional experience. If so, how would Satan transition that because they don't go? He can't. He's the father of lies.

It's the validation of emotions that what we're feeling, that's the goal. I talk often about being a postmodern, which is to say a post-Christian culture, but now it can be described as post-truth.

Our culture has made it palatable to reject believing in God, without realizing the ramification that if you reject God, you reject truth, and if you reject truth, you can't have any education because the goal of education is to teach truth. This will eventually lead to the breakdown of society because all society is founded on the existence of moral law. Without this foundational moral law, everyone does what they want, and society breaks down.

Then how do you live your life? What do you substitute for truth? Consequently, it results in self-promoting, self-aggrandizement, self-actualization; having the right to do whatever you want to achieve your emotional goals, which means anything is justifiable. However, ultimately no one can live this way. For example, if we go into the hospital, we expect the doctor to give us the truth on what caused the disease and what the cure is. There is truth. The same is true with the illness of our negative emotions, God gives us the truth so we may be cured. God knows exactly where you are. You're still in the palm of His hand. You're still eternally valuable to Him. If you toss out truth, which I think our culture has done, you toss out the very thing that will give us safety, security, and peace. We see it all around us in our culture. We are grasping at anything that we think makes us feel significant at the time. So, what do we do now?

Thankfully, God has placed eternity in the heart of every human being (Ecclesiastes 3:11). Every person still is created in the image of God and ultimately understands deep in his or her heart that there is a God. We are created with a God consciousness, our soul. There is an imprint on our heart. We don't always understand it. but it's there. No matter how far we drift, there's nothing we can get ourselves into that we're beyond the reach of the Holy Spirit of God to open our understanding. God allows us to experience some of those awful negative things in life because some of us have to fall that far before we will listen and open our heart and mind. And that is okay, because the ultimate goal for God is our heart. There have been times and seasons throughout human history where God has shown that He is still master of it all.

As Greg states, each person is ultimately trying to achieve their highest quality of life. As people age, they understand that their highest quality of life is not found in a standard of living, but having peace in their hearts, which can only be achieved by living Greg's repeated paradigm of rational, healthy, wise, and right. It's the practicality of how we should address negative emotions in each of our individual lives. In addition to that, there are key philosophical, psychological, sociological truths within this book that our society and culture needs, because this is the underpinning of our moral and cultural fabric. Our culture has forgotten who we are or is aggressively rejecting who we are. From our founding, not everyone was Christian, but nearly everyone had a Christian understanding. They knew that no matter what they got themselves into, there were guiding parameters out there, and they were largely Christian. Today, Christianity is not only no longer at the head of the table, in some places it's not even at the table. In the public university, for example, nearly everything is accepted and promoted except Christianity. Over time, our culture has systematically removed foundational truths in our families and in our schools. Even many Christians today have a rough understanding of the main Bible stories, like Samson, or Daniel in the lion's den, but they can't tell you what it means for them today. It's just a cool story. They don't know how to apply it. When people get into trouble today, what's their backstop? Nothing. Not everyone in the Greatest Generation were believers, but they had grown up understanding Judeo-Christian values. I think that undergirded a lot of them as they went off to war. Now we have radically different values, and the consequences are obvious.

The key, as Greg states, is to challenge our mental models. We all know that we can evaluate choices according to the grid of rational, healthy, wise, and right. But we need to go further and seek with all of our hearts and find objective truth. My thoughts are not God's thoughts. So how do I learn God's thoughts? How do I find objective truth, truth that is rational, healthy, wise, and right? By starting with the Word of God, the Bible.

Dr. Rex M. Rogers
www.rexmrogers.com
www.youtube.com/@DrRexRogers

Preface

I wrote this book to help as many people as possible have as few negative emotions as possible. I have over 50 years of experience being neurotic. I have watched myself be consumed with burning so much energy on things I can't control; as well as burning a lot of energy trying to reconcile in my mind why what I think of myself is different than what others think of me. If you don't struggle with these experiences, then this book is not for you, and that's okay! I have worked with thousands of people individually and in groups helping them overcome their emotions, as well as equip them to help others overcome their own emotions. My prayer is the Lord uses me to help as many as possible until we can finally experience the full peace that surpasses all understanding.

Acknowledgements

I want to thank my wife, who is the most loving, supportive, caring, and servant-hearted person this side of glory. I want to thank my children, my grandchildren, my great grandchildren, and all generations that come after me. This book is part of my legacy I leave to you. Most of all, I want to thank my First Love and Fiancé, how can I give thanks, for all that You have done for me? I love You. With all my heart, I love You.

Introduction

You can't impart what you don't possess. – Bill Johnson

Bill Johnson is the senior pastor of Bethel Church in Redding, California. His ministry, as well as the worship music produced by Bethel, has touched millions of lives, including mine. When I meditate on this quote, it takes me back to the first time I heard Bill speak this truth and its profound impact on me. This defining moment, this epiphany, occurred during the most difficult season of my life. I had been in the middle of a painful divorce following my emotional affair. Although it was one of the most challenging seasons of my life, it would also turn out to be one of the most spiritually and emotionally powerful chapters. Bill's point was simple but profound: we don't possess the authority to grant counsel or advice to others that we ourselves do not apply. This statement, however, has a much deeper and richer meaning to it. Allow me to explain what I mean. There are two levels to our existence, our conscious awareness, and our unconscious. There is a "surface" level of existence which encompasses our present awareness of our mental, emotional, and behavioral selves. We exchange advice and ideas with one another freely to find the optimal ways in which to increase our personal standard of living; to make our lives easier and more pleasurable, with the end goal being the maximizing our sensory adventure. It doesn't matter if neither person has *applied* the advice or counsel because the point of the exchange is to share practical ideas (financial, parenting, etc.). However, when so-called authority figures dole out advice that they themselves do not abide by, such as a broke financial planner, or an out-of-shape physical trainer or nutritionist, we can separate the message from the messenger because there is a high probability what they advise is still true.

Then there is the deeper level of existence which involve matters of the heart and the soul. This is where we strive for meaning and purpose, with the end goal being peace and rest. This is what Bill Johnson's quote addresses. However, in matters of the heart and soul, the message and the messenger are one. This is because the truths at this level are transformed into *wisdom, insight, discernment, and understanding*. This is assuming, of course, what they are advising passes the test of Rational, Healthy, Wise, and Right (discussed later). We know in our hearts these words of counsel and insight contain objective truths, but these truths have been fortified with the negative personal elements of failure, weaknesses, pain, and the exposure of fears and insecurities. The exhaustive process of merging the objective truths with our negative personal elements into one inseparable DNA structure of wisdom, insight, discernment, and understanding is the proof of our tenacity and resilience in choosing to abandon the façade of our emotional self-preservation to achieve the true wealth of life: meaning. (I understand, read it again). As you read this book, this truth will become more and more clear and more and more true. This sentence summarizes my personal journey; this book walks you through how I experienced it. Only after we have achieved *meaning* can we experience the coveted state of peace and finally be at rest.

INTRODUCTION

My goal in writing this book is to equip you with information and insight for both levels of your existence in order to achieve this deeper peace and meaning. As I explain later, our emotional experiences our divided into present-tense emotional experiences and deeper, more fulfilling emotional experiences related to our overall quality of life. Furthermore, you will see both levels of existence as intertwined and unable to exist independently from one another. This book will be the inauguration of the journey into your deeper levels, just as Bill Johnson's quote was the point of inauguration for my journey. As I tell all my clients, everything I share has first been run through my own personal journey. I will be transparent, honest, and at times blunt. I am telling you in advance to cover any negative emotions or offense that may occur throughout this book. The reason is that I myself had to choose to transform every hurt or offense into an invitation to uncover into a deep insight into myself, rather than blame others or obfuscate. However, if you are not emotionally ready to do the same and open your own invitations, then stop here, and put the book back on the shelf. It's okay. I mean that with all my heart, it's okay. I believe you want to "go there"; you just need to find your own way to prepare for it. I cannot over-emphasize enough that if you are ready to begin this journey, you must choose right now to leave your well-worn magnifying glass at the beginning of this journey and instead pick up your untarnished mirror. Know this: the magnifying glass that was used so often to examine others and sooth yourself would have eventually turned you bitter and left your soul empty once you realize that a lot more energy should have been spent on examining self over others. Whereas what the unused mirror will reflect, at first glance, will embarrass and agitate, compelling you to look away, but in the end, your reflection will be the proof you now have meaning, peace, and rest when you look into the eyes of . . . you.

Chapter 1
The Stories We Tell Ourselves

The Status Quo

As I age and reflect on my life, the memories that have always stood out slowly become the defining moments forming who I am today. These defining moments are the foundational pillars of the various careers I have held as a pastor, professor, counselor, coach, and consultant. I will share many of these moments throughout this book, not in chronological order but as they fit into the flow of the book. The first of these pivotal moments was early on in grade school. My dad worked for General Motors for his entire career. He was a member of the last of the "30-years and out" generation, where you worked for 30 years and retired to hopefully live happily ever after. I remember several occasions when he would come home and discuss leadership, management, and how he felt the plant was run. Looking back at who he was, I am a little surprised at how my down-to-earth, blue-collar dad (who was never in management) was so intrigued about organizational aspects beyond his individual role in the company. I remember a specific time he shared with me some of his knowledge. One time, he talked to me about a simple theory of organizational change and how it was impacting his plant in Kalamazoo, MI. General Motors, like most car companies at the time, was attempting to adapt its overall business model to mimic the Japanese method, which had received remarkable success in the auto industry. The specific topic of change he was teaching me was organizational in nature, where management was attempting to change processes and systems within the plant. He drew two vertical lines on a sheet of paper and in the middle of those lines he wrote the words "status quo." On the left side of these vertical lines, he wrote "promoters" and on the right side he wrote "resistors". He described the status quo as the current system of processes and procedures that everyone was accustomed to. However, once GM started experiencing the pain from the Japanese auto industry stealing market share, they were forced to assess and improve their status quo. New strategies developed out of a new vision, and with these new strategies came changes to standing processes and procedures. The promoters of the change (leadership and management) wanted to become more effective and efficient. The resistors (the employees) were those who liked things the way they were. My dad's goal was not to teach me who he thought was right, but about the process of change itself and the most effective way to enact it. For example, should leadership and management use their positions of authority and expertise to force the change? Or should they just keep the status quo so as to not to create conflict and potentially instigate a strike? What was the best way to move the bars (vertical lines) and create a new status quo? From what I remember, the organization attempted both paths to little or no avail. He taught me about the concepts of "what" and "how", with *what* being the best decision of what should be done as far as processes and procedures, the *how* is the way we communicate the what and is all about relationships and human emotions. In other words, how do we build relationships and trust in order to motivate the resistors to switch their allegiance to effectively become promoters of the new system? This conversation was the defining moment that introduced me to the topic of organizational leadership.

Everything is Changing

That conversation with my dad was revelatory. My eyes were suddenly open to the process of change, and I soon saw it happening all around me. I tuned in to a constant chatter about change, either positively or negatively. As a kid, I would see wives lament because their husbands weren't changing, and husbands staunchly defending the fact they don't need to. I observed the constant prattle of politicians who see themselves as the saviors who bring needed change while others see themselves as the heroic defenders of things that remain set in stone. I would often ask myself, "Why would anybody want to change the status quo to begin with?" And "If someone wanted to change the status quo, why would people resist?" I began to examine the nature of change itself. I started to think to myself, *What if those who promoted change were wrong. What if it should be resisted?* And on the contrary, what if those who resisted change were wrong? But most importantly I wondered, *how in the world do you know who's right or who's wrong?*

The same principles and questions concerning organizational change can be applied to how people view change themselves, both internally and externally. As I grew, I started to observe how some people struggle with their own personal growth. Those who talk about starting the new diet tomorrow yet never seem to get in shape. Or those who preached about financial freedom yet racked up more and more credit card debt each month. Likewise, as a teenager and young adult, I became painfully aware of my own lack of success in personal growth. I wanted to grow and change but struggled greatly to actually make the change permanent. The entire topic of change became so intriguing to me. If we wanted to change, and we had 100% control over making that change, what in the world would be stopping us from changing? I definitely *wanted* to grow and change, but I also definitely *wanted* to stay the same. When faced with a moment where I had the perfect opportunity to choose to do something different (the change I wanted), I had this driving energy inside of me to do what I have always done (the very thing I didn't want to do). What in the world was this all about? When I made the right choice, I felt great, and when I made the wrong choice, I felt horrible. I wanted to quit doing things like drinking and using drugs and wanted to start doing better in school, but I also wanted to continue to party and wanted to avoid doing homework! After experiencing this paradox multiple times, I wondered why, at the very moment of decision, my emotions were pushing me in both directions. More than that, I wondered about the emotional obstacles inside of all of us that resist change, even when we've already included that we want to make this change. These questions became the seeds and the foundational growth in my various careers. In a way, they became my calling. I found that there weren't only positive emotions that motivated me to change (e.g. confidence in doing better and being successful), but also negative emotions that resisted the change (e.g. frustration over quitting what I loved to do: party, which possibly meant the loss of my friend group). I also discovered that, when I was willing to look closer, I could see the negative emotions revealed deeper insights about myself (insecurities, fears, and need for validation).

Reframing Negative Emotions

In this book, I will walk you through how to uncover the deeper meanings behind the negative emotions that resist change. These negative emotions may come up in a variety of ways, such as the emotions we feel when we fail to change. For example, the shame and anger some feel when they've committed to getting in shape on January 1st, and come December, the scale hasn't budged an inch. Or maybe it's the negative emotions we feel when others point out our need for change (defensiveness) or for failing to actually change (embarrassment). As humans, we naturally want to experience as few negative emotions as possible, but I have discovered three simple truths that have fundamentally changed my relationship with negative emotions. One, many negative emotions get a bad rap. Two, avoiding negative emotions is the very thing that keeps them alive and makes them thrive. Three, turning around and facing our negative emotions as we walk right into the heart of them is where we find the richness of life itself.

If we feel bad about something we have done or are doing, we still habitually tell ourselves stories to frame the negative emotions as "bad" and dismiss them. When someone tells us we need to change, they just make us feel bad about ourselves, so we attack them out loud or in our minds for doing so. If we experience negative emotions from our environment (others, society, or God, for example), we tell ourselves that if only our environment changes, our negative emotions will change. While throughout my life I have personally learned to practice the three truths above and have worked hard to equip others to do the same, I have noticed just the opposite movement in society. There has been an increase in vilifying of negative emotions over the last 20-30 years. There is not only the goal of diluting internal negative emotions at all costs, but we have begun to frame any external force that produces negative emotions as bad and morally corrupt.

I have a polar opposite approach to the environmental sources of negative emotions. I am convinced our negative emotions contain a treasure trove of knowledge we must simply tap into. What's more, gaining that information and understanding it is the only way to create lasting, healthy change and the only way to find true richness in our lives. I have also found those who refuse to walk this road fail to grow, or change at such a slow rate, they ultimately amplify their negative emotions and never experience the richness that ensues when one grows at a soul level. This is why the subtitle of this book is what it is: *Unlock the inner strength behind your negative emotions.* As Aragorn made the literal world-changing decision to go into the mountains to face his fears by confronting the army of the dead in the *Lord of the Rings* movie *The Return of the King*, we must have the courage to walk into the darkness of our negative emotions to become the healthiest and most powerful we have ever been. I am inviting you to have the courage not to avoid your negative emotions, but to walk right into them with an open mind and open heart. This book is written for those who have the courage to no longer avoid the truth hidden within their negative emotions.

In Search of the Highest Quality of Life

We grow up telling ourselves that we need to be a certain way, have a certain standard of living, have certain kinds of relationships, and have our environment treat us in a certain way to live the highest quality of life, or in other words, be fully alive. The early church father, St. Irenaeus, stated "The glory of God is man fully alive."

Everyone has a vision of what their lives would look like if they were fully alive (vision of our desired standard of living, if all relationships were great, meaning and purpose in life). Creating and writing this story is the core of the human experience and can be a very good thing overall. However, we also go through numerous experiences where we see our stories were flawed, so we continually adjust that story as we grow. After all, the definition of what *fully alive* looks like matures over time. When I was a child, I envisioned being a police officer. As a teenager, I pictured being great at sports and dating the hottest girls. As an adult, I pictured myself changing the world through my ministry as a pastor. Sadly, many of us still experience a discouraging gap between what we are experiencing and what we would experience if we achieved our highest quality of life. My focus is helping people, in both counseling and coaching, to not only unpack the reasons why they have been unsuccessful in closing that gap but also help them develop critical thinking skills in unveiling the values, beliefs, and opinions that created the story in the first place. If our goal as humans is to achieve our version of the highest quality of life, then we are truly pursuing an overall emotional experience better than our current state. That is our macro goal, an emotional experience. To achieve this macro goal, we constantly pursue smaller micro goals of improving our emotional experience in the here and now, such as eating, drinking, watching a movie, or accomplishing a task. The goal is the emotional experience, and we do things every day to achieve our vision of that goal.

Emotional Goals and Behavioral Paths

Everything we do is an attempt to achieve an emotional goal.
We are either trying to increase our quality of life by doing something that produces positive emotions or changing something to avoid negative emotions. It is important to differentiate our emotional goals from the paths (behaviors, actions, choices) we take to achieve our emotional goals. Now, the root of our emotional goals tends to be healthy and beautiful. The problem is not the emotional goal we are trying to achieve but the paths we take to achieve those emotional goals. These paths come in the form of our choices, actions, behaviors, responses, and habits. Think through one habit you have that you want to change. Why do you want to change it? If it's causing you problems, why do you keep doing it? Because you are trying to achieve some emotional goal (experience) and either haven't found another path, or are more committed to your current path, even if you know these paths are causing you problems or causing other people in your life problems. Ironically, even though you know this to be true, you get defensive and upset when others point out the need for you to change! I should use the pronoun "we", but I'm sure you are okay with me exposing you a little bit like this because you know it's true.

I frequently hear people argue over their paths, staunchly defending their preferred path, when the truth is that there are several different paths to achieve our agreed-upon emotional goals. For example, spouses argue about where they should go out to eat. What are the goals? To feel full and to have a pleasurable experience when the food passes over our palette, accompanied by someone we love. We burn way too much emotional energy over paths sometimes! Take a moment and examine yourself to see how this applies. Our day-to-day behaviors illustrate how we achieve our surface emotional goals.

We eat to *feel* full, drink to *not feel* thirsty, shower to *feel* clean, pet our dog to *feel* their soft fur and *feel* love, go to the store to *feel* secure because we have food for our family, and watch a movie to *feel* a temporary escape from the stress of our lives. When we realize there are several paths to achieve our emotional goals, we can loosen our emotional grip on a particular path, especially if that path causes issues for us or others around us.

You probably have heard the phrase, "the end justifies the means." This phrase means that it is okay to do whatever it takes, even if it's wrong, to accomplish your goal. But we all know that the end doesn't justify the means. While the end goal is good, that doesn't automatically apply to the means it takes to get there. The application of this saying and the principle I am putting forth in this chapter are the same: separate the goal (end) from the path (means), and we need to evaluate the path (means) we use to accomplish our end (emotional goals). I'm assuming we all agree with this and are aware we should change some of our paths (means), such as our choices, actions, behaviors, responses, and habits; and yet the question remains, "Why is it so difficult to change once and for all and relinquish all ineffective paths? Why do we return to them?" As you and I sit here today, we can do a quick scan of our paths and life circumstances and identify several areas where we would like our lives to be improved. These changes would be described and listed in two columns: *changes in ourselves* and *changes in our environment*. What is your strategy to make these changes in each of these columns? What is your strategy for changing yourself? What is your strategy for changing your environment? If you believe you have a good strategy, but your success rate of change in each column is low, then what stories are you telling yourself to explain why it's not working?

As humans, we are more committed to what's familiar than what is healthy. Even though it may be dysfunctional, we are more comfortable with what we are used to (our habits), and it takes a lot of work to change those habits. Further, we are all very committed to emotional self-preservation from negative emotions, such as the feeling we are failing overall or are a "loser" because we can't change, which is normal and very human. Even if we have already committed to making certain changes but are unsuccessful, we can get frustrated and discouraged. Helping you become successful is the subject of an innumerable number of books, and many have great techniques. I hope to add to a list of techniques to assist you. My focus is trying to help you better understand the role negative emotions play in the process. They don't "feel" good, but that's the point! Sure, there is a way to get rid of them – by changing! When we don't change and we know we should change, we get defensive and commit what is called the *fundamental attribution error*. Attribution error is a psychological term that states we attribute other's failures and shortcomings to who they are as a person. In other words, their character is flawed. But when explaining the reason for our lack of success, we blame our environment and circumstances. Very rarely do we blame ourselves. The goal (reducing negative emotions) is good, the path (defensiveness and criticism) is bad. Instead of using the term "bad," I want to equip you with a grid of evaluation that will be used to self-assess our paths.

Objective Truth: Rational, Healthy, Wise, and Right (RHWR)

Our minds are set up in a think-feel-do linear process. We think about the immediate situation, gather our emotions about it, and then respond to it as we see fit. We do what we do, we feel what we feel because we think what we think. What we think is simply information and details about the situation, but what we feel about it is another matter. We evaluate the facts, which creates an opinion, which then creates an emotion. When we evaluate our quality of life (think), whether it be micro (here and now), or macro (overall habits, accomplishments, and standard of living), and if our interpretation is negative, it produces negative emotions. We use those emotions to enact a change to our micro and macro quality of life. In the micro, we oftentimes are so focused on feeling something different we impulsively just *do* without assessing the paths (choices, actions, and responses) before we act. Our goal is always good, but if we choose the wrong path, it is going to cause problems.

    We choose our paths for a variety of reasons, which I will address in the next chapter, but for now, let's begin the process of how to evaluate why we chose our paths. The easiest paths to evaluate are the behaviors we already know we want to change. What is it about that path that makes it bad? Is the path irrational? When you commit the fundamental attribution error, you are being irrational by attributing your weaknesses to your circumstances at the time and blaming other's weaknesses on their flawed character. Is your path unhealthy? Raising your voice at others and name-calling is not healthy. Is your path unwise? You really want your children to have a great Christmas, but you go into debt to achieve that goal. Is your path wrong? You hold others to a standard of behavior that you yourself don't live up to, and you make excuses for yourself, again resorting to the fundamental attribution error. Are you perhaps experiencing negative emotions because of what I am suggesting? We can narrow our behaviors, choices, actions, and responses into the following categories: rational or irrational, healthy or unhealthy, wise or unwise, right or wrong. For this application, I will refer to this grid as RHWR. By doing this, you can understand the unwanted behavior differently and assign a different degree of importance to the unwanted behavior. For example, a behavior that is wrong (as opposed to right), carries a heavier weight of impact than a behavior that is unwise. Doing something wrong creates more negative emotion because it's a moral choice, as opposed to an unwise choice. You can't change all your unwanted behaviors at once, so prioritize them according to this grid and focus on the more heavily weighted ones first. Additionally, when you consider alternative paths, think of paths that would be more rational, healthy, wise, or right.

While doing this, practice simultaneously identifying the emotional goal you are trying to achieve. In each unwanted behavior, ask yourself, "When I do that behavior, what am I trying to feel?" Be as specific as possible; find the perfect word. Then assess why the path you chose did not pass the RHWR grid. Own it and even apologize for it if you need to. Then brainstorm and come up with as many RHWR paths as you can that would accomplish that same emotional goal in the future. The process helps equip your brain with alternatives in the future so it doesn't default to habitual non-RHWR behavior. This works well for the micro process. Now, let's discuss the macro process.

What do you yearn to be different about your life? Your standard of living? Your accomplishments? Your career? When you answer these questions, you are choosing paths. Some of you might have answered the first question by wanting to feel different (less anxiety), which is fine, but for now, let's stick to tangible quality-of-life changes. Once you define these paths, describe the emotional goal you are trying to achieve via that path. For example, earning a bachelor's degree is not the goal; it is the path we choose to take to achieve the emotional goal of feeling more accomplished, or it may be a sub-goal to the path of getting a job that pays significantly more, in order to achieve the emotional goal of an increased standard of living. When we understand it in this way, we realize that there are several paths we can take to achieve our true goal, which is emotional.

Now, let's explore our deeper emotional goals of feeling accepted, feeling like we belong, feeling secure, feeling successful and significant, and feeling value and worth in our identity. What paths are you taking to achieve these emotional goals? What are your paths of response when someone blocks your current path to achieve an emotional goal? Every time someone corrects us, confronts us, insults us, teases us, etc., our emotional goal of feeling secure and significant is blocked, so we then choose a path to correct that person to reopen the path of our emotional goal. Even if we outwardly disagree with them, inwardly, our negative emotions greatly increase as we try to reconcile the paradox between what that person thinks of us versus what we think of ourselves. Humans desire approval and acceptance from others. As a result, we then choose internal responses by continuing to argue with them in our minds, and/or disqualify them by insulting their character or judging their motives (fundamental attribution error). If we are successful, while we don't change their opinion of us, we do nullify the emotional impact of their opinion. This, in turn, removes them as an obstacle to our emotional goal… to feel accepted and good about ourselves. Reflect on the stories you've told yourself about others over the years to achieve your emotional goals. Consider how many of these paths would pass the RHWR grid.

Likewise, we use various behavioral paths to procure our emotional goals using food, liquids, producers of dopamine, relationships, activities, and experiences. Be honest with yourself enough and differentiate between which paths are RHWR and which paths are not. Can you clearly link each of your paths (habits) to the emotional goal you are trying to achieve? Choosing non-RHWR paths is the plight of the human experience, and soon, this choice becomes a habit. That leads us to an even greater battle: owning it. I'm assuming you thought I was going to say that the greatest battle was transitioning from a non-RHWR path to a path that is RHWR, which is certainly another great battle! But first, the greater tussle is owning the fact that the current path doesn't pass the RHWR test and truly being willing to change. Can we first let our defenses down and *openly* own the fact that our path is not RHWR? My heart goes out to clients because many people find themselves pursuing emotional goals that originate from deep, profound hurt. Rejection, verbal, emotional, and physical abuse, trauma, neglect, and the like have created deep emotional holes in the hearts of individuals. Instead of pouring their energies into the micro emotional goals (day-to-day happiness and enjoyment), these individuals are desperately trying to climb out of the deeper and greater abyss of negative emotions and achieve the emotional goals of security, safety, trust, happiness, or belonging. They deeply want to solidify their emotional foundation so they can finally begin building and working on increasing their quality of life. Until then, they are trying to achieve the emotional goals of *not* feeling certain emotions through non-RHWR paths, which creates a downward spiral because these paths, while maybe offering temporary relief, creates more problems for them and for others around them.

    A frequently used example of goal versus path is when someone experiencing a great deal of stress chooses the path of abusing alcohol to achieve the emotional goal of less stress/more peace. The emotional goal is good, but the path the person takes to achieve the emotional goal is unhealthy. Abusing alcohol to decrease negative emotions is one of the clearest examples of not only using an unhealthy path to achieve an emotional goal but also demonstrates the paradox of someone wanting to make an obvious change to their behavior, but greatly struggling to do so. While the solution may seem obvious, many advise this person to just "stop." My approach to this individual would begin with first trusting that he/she truly does not want to use this path to help with the current stresses they are experiencing. Secondly, using the principle of goal/path theory, I would help him/her see that the goal isn't to quit drinking but to reduce stress, and using the path of abusing alcohol to get there is unhealthy. By doing this, we discuss several other paths they could use to achieve this same goal that would pass the test of rational, healthy, wise, and right. However, sometimes, even after equipping a person this way, they may still struggle to switch paths. Why? Is it because this person is not committed? Does he/she really want to change? I trust their motives, and frankly, I try very hard not to ever judge other's motives. I find it to be dangerous, offensive, and judgmental, and it doesn't help solve the problem. It's wasted energy. So then, what could the reason be why they are not switching paths?

    I start by explaining to the client that every irrational, unhealthy, unwise, and wrong path we choose to achieve an emotional goal *has its own emotional rewards attached* to the path itself. Simply, there is an immediate emotional reward to a non-RHWR path, or else we would have never chosen it to begin with! It's crucial to understand that the non-RHWR paths have their own emotional rewards attached, and if we discontinue these paths, we will experience some kind of loss. In our example, when a person switches to a RHWR path from the non-RHWR path of drinking alcohol to relieve stress, they realize they must now forfeit the numbing (or even pleasant) feeling alcohol elicits. By switching paths, they encounter a type of emotional loss. Despite knowing the cost of abusing alcohol both physically, emotionally, and relationally, the numbing effects of alcohol may still hold them captive. Why? Because we all suffer from myopia. Myopia is simply a synonym for near-sightedness. We clearly see objects near to us, but objects further away appear blurry. Symbolically, the emotional reward right in front of us is clear as crystal. Conversely, the consequences remain blurry or hidden. Since the positive feeling is "closer," we are more likely to go and grab it. The emotional intelligence (EI) skills that describe this process are *impulse control* and *delay of gratification*. We start to develop these skills from our very first breath. In infancy, we express our emotions and immediately start the goal/path process. We cry because we are hungry and want to feel full. However, sometimes we cried just for attention, affirming our emotional goal of affection. This is one of the first big challenges for parents, who are responsible for developing the EI skills of impulse control and delay of gratification. If they know we don't have a need, they need to let us "cry it out" and control our impulses. If they don't succeed in this battle (because they have their own emotional goal: to feel comfort by comforting us), then they *enable* this non-RHWR behavior, prompting the baby to try it again. When we impulsively choose non-RHWR paths, we are setting a precedent for our future success, but also, we hurt those around us because they become obligated to respond to our choice. During the proverbial "terrible two's," we encounter the struggle of controlling our outbursts and impulse control, such as pushing our siblings or pinching our preschool friends. These proclivities follow us all the way through our challenging adolescent years. We struggle to restrain our impulses in relation to our teachers and parents, saying "no" to peer pressure and choosing to do homework and chores before watching TV or playing on our phones. I tell parents to use the phrase, "Duty and Discipline before Dopamine" as an easy reminder for their teens to memorize to start to train themselves in impulse control and delay of gratification. These same lessons extend to college, learning how to have a successful relationship with a roommate or boyfriend/girlfriend, being able to communicate effectively with our spouses, and/or being consistent in exercising and eating healthy. We eventually develop impulse control and delayed gratification, or we would still be throwing temper tantrums on the ground and slapping people silly when we get angry with them. However, as with any skill, there are varying levels of skill development. Some are novices, some have a working knowledge, and others are masters. What is your skill level? The answer is given by your degree of success in stopping non-RHWR habits and forming new, RHWR habits. Controlling your impulse of wanting to continue to go back to the non-RHWR goals will help this stop-start process.

Love and Marriage

One of the most significant tests of managing impulses and gratification is in relationships. This is where the human desire to achieve emotional goals is at its highest, and negative emotions peak when those goals are blocked. I have worked with many men and women who participate in certain sexual behaviors, whether it is promiscuity, pornography, emotional or physical affairs, etc., to achieve the emotional goals of love, security, and admiration. These couples, who have been affected by immoral sexual behaviors, must overcome enormous obstacles in their healing process by first delving into their emotional goal and the path they chose to achieve it. I believe that no married person sets out to engage in immoral sexual behaviors intentionally, and it is often an emotional goal they are trying to achieve. For men, this emotional goal is often significance. If he feels he is not achieving that goal, he chooses various paths to achieve that goal. He may pour all his energy into his career or sports, but for most men, their main path to significance is to be admired and desired by their girlfriend or wife. The drive to achieve this emotional goal is found in the opposite sex. Seeking significance through a relationship with the opposite sex is a major factor leading up to men and immoral sexual behaviors. Like alcohol, there is an immediate reward, which can lead to disastrous consequences. Most women pursue a variety of paths to achieve the emotional goal of security (or safety). While most of the paths involve relationships with several friends and loved ones, the main path is via the path of her relationship with her husband. Women fall into affairs when their husbands are not meeting the emotional goal of security. Security has several forms, such as affection, conversation, transparency and openness by her husband, and of course, the stability of her family, as well as her financial stability. Suppose her spouse doesn't meet one or more of these emotional goals, and someone else comes along and starts meeting those goals. In that case, it develops into an inappropriate emotional attachment and may culminate sexually. The irony is many of these paths end up backfiring and leaving them even farther away from their initial goal. I share this information from my own experience of my emotional affair and the consequences it caused.

The failure to meet one another's emotional goals doesn't just happen overnight. It may begin with what initially seemed like a healthy goal, which over time, spiraled into an obsession. For men, it may be their careers, sports, or (believe it or not) video games, and for women, it could be their relationships with family, children, or friends. The failure to meet these emotional needs often lies in a lack of communication, by either a lack of it, or through having poor skills in problem resolution. Many problem-solving discussions escalate into arguments because we possess poor communication skills coupled with our own insecurities. We feel exposed and attacked. We defend ourselves while lashing out at our partner and in the process, we hurt one another.

Anger towards your spouse or significant other usually stems from them speaking or doing something that increases your negative emotions. In other words, how they "made" you feel. Many men use the word "disrespected" while women describe feeling "emotionally unsafe." Anger is an attempt to get the other person to apologize and change how they come across to us, so we no longer feel the threat to our emotional goal. The resulting emotion is often not created from disagreement, but from *how* our spouse talks to us. Every couple has topics and problems they need to work through, but the reason why the emotions escalate so much is not because of our differing opinions, but because of *the way* we disagree with one another gets interpreted as a threat to our security or significance. Therefore, we brilliantly use the path of increasing our intensity, and/or dismissing, ridiculing, or mocking their opinion, and insulting their character and motives. Like I said, brilliant. Now, because of their confrontation with us, we see them as blocking our main emotional goals and we use anger towards them as a way to remove them (via the same foolish paths) from blocking our emotional goals.

If the hurt continues and the anger isn't resolved, we begin to withdraw from one another, resulting in abandoning the emotional goals we vowed to each other at the altar. If this continues for a long enough period, each spouse may begin entertaining other paths to meet these emotional goals. Upon realizing the use of alternative paths, more criticism and anger can follow. Women may start complaining about the video games, the golf, the friends, the job, and if she notices any relational engagement with a female "friend," the gloves come off. Because men are so dependent on being admired by the opposite sex, they fall more easily into sexual immorality. King Solomon was okay with having a thousand wives, but the wives only had one husband! The lie is the greater number of women a man has desiring him, the greater he feels admired and desired, which then gets linked to the most addictive drug: sex. Our spouses are NEVER to blame for our immoral path choices, but if the path to our emotional goals is blocked, we foolishly make the mistake of trying to find other paths.

There is a verse in the Bible that says, "Remember, the sins of some people are obvious, leading them to certain judgment. But there are others whose sins will not be revealed until later (1 Timothy 5:24)."[1] Men are more easily exposed because they use outward, immoral sins (paths) to meet their emotional goals, while women use more culturally acceptable paths to achieve their emotional goals. The immoral sexual behaviors are exposed and broadcast publicly, but only after much time, much counseling,

---

[1] *Holy Bible*, New Living Translation, copyright © 1996, 2004, 2015 by Tyndale House Foundation.

and much healing do the sins of the wife become revealed. When I say sin, I mean her own mistakes in the marriage. Both are equally culpable for the state of their marriage, but only the man is culpable for the immoral behavior. Women rightly point out, "We are both to blame for the state of our marriage, but I never went outside of our marriage!" Because of this truth, it is sometimes very hard to transition the focus from the offense itself onto the topic that led to it in the first place: the failure to meet one another's needs.

Furthermore, even though the wife may not have turned to another man to meet her emotional needs, it doesn't necessarily mean the paths she did use are more rational, healthy, wise, or right. Any alternate path we use to meet our marital emotional needs is not rational, healthy, wise, or right. We can't excuse ourselves by lamenting the fact that our spouses are not meeting our marital needs as justification for using those alternate paths. Using the paths discussed above may appear to be less offensive. However, this may make it more difficult for some women to acknowledge the need to make a change. Therefore, it's obviously easier to continue that path with little to no negative emotion (from consequences) motivating her back to the RHWR path of her husband. Think for a moment about the differences between pornography and romance novels. The former is visual and offensive, but the latter can still be just as pornographic but in the form of "story" and relational romance. Is the social stigma attached to romance novels (or daytime dramas) lower than the social stigma attached to pornography? Both are still immoral, but you can see how 1 Timothy 5:24 is applied here.

Those Beautiful RTC Patients

By far, one of the most difficult but rewarding jobs I have held was working as the Director of a Residential Treatment Center (RTC) at a behavioral health hospital. A RTC is a long-term, inpatient hospitalization for adolescents who have had one or more short-term (acute) hospitalizations for suicidal ideation or attempts, homicidal ideation (much less frequent), or active psychosis (equally less frequent). If the short-term hospitalizations are not helping the patient stabilize, they are referred to the RTC for a longer-term stay of roughly six weeks to six months. Almost every teenager admitted has trauma or a loss of relationship with one or both of their biological parents. When I was first hired at the hospital, I was a therapist in the girl's unit of the RTC. Many don't like working with teenage girls because of all the drama and cattiness but I loved it and loved them. I developed a tender heart for these girls.

As you might imagine, the stories I listened to were heartbreaking. I don't believe I need to share the specifics of the stories because you probably have an idea of the types of traumas these children and young women had to endure. Besides all forms of abuse and neglect, these children/teenagers must face the fact that one or both biological parents have chosen to be nonexistent for a variety of reasons. This is an additional deep form of trauma for them. The emotional needs these young ones and teenagers are desperately trying to achieve were much more foundational than the emotional needs/wants you and I desire to obtain. The same truth applies to them as it does to us (everything we do is trying to achieve an emotional goal). Many of the adolescent females would self-harm to cope with their experiences and achieve their emotional goals. What specific emotional goals were they trying to achieve through the self-harm technique of cutting? In my work with these dear girls, they cut for three main reasons. The most common seemed to be related to the heaviness of their deep pain bubbling inside. Cutting themselves created a symbolic feeling of releasing their pain through bleeding. Another emotional goal cutting would achieve would be temporary relief of the constant, intense pain they felt in their hearts by transferring that pain to a different location. Finally, some were so emotionally numb or "dead" from their life experiences and disappointments they just wanted to achieve the emotional goal of feeling something, anything! The psychological undercurrent is profound, but the foundational principle is always the same: everything we do is trying to achieve an emotional goal. Some of the patients would even swallow batteries or other objects, rub their feces on their walls, and find different ways of harming themselves.

Another path used to meet emotional goals was gender dysphoria. Contrary to what one might think, this path was used far more often by the girls than the boys. The ratio of girls to boys who became transgender was upwards of 20:1. Why are so many more girls experimenting with becoming transgender? One common trait that transcended many of the girls was the timing of their transition after some form of sexualized trauma. I believe they chose this path in an attempt to achieve their goal of security and safety. By becoming a boy, they now assumed the identity of the gender that hurt them, making them peers. This transition now meant they were on the same level of power, even *feeling* stronger as a boy. Furthermore, they may have believed that by being a boy, they weren't seen as much of a target by abusers as if they had remained a girl. I realize the behavior of cutting is very puzzling to many people. We can't understand why this is such a popular form of self-harm among girls. You may have marveled many times at some of the behaviors of others, like many of the behaviors promoted in our current culture. Likewise, many of my clients are confused, embarrassed, and marvel at their own behaviors, not being able to explain the rationale behind why they do what they do. I often tell clients that one of the goals I try to achieve is to take the mystery out of why we do what we do. There is always a (psycho)logical reason for why we do what we do. Apply the emotional goal/path principle to every one of these behaviors and you will immediately start to see the obvious link between the behavior and the emotional goal. I worked with a brilliant, sweet man who was addicted to diaper pornography (where the adult actors dress as infants and then engage in sexual acts). The (psycho)logical reason? He had a huge vacuum in his heart because he never bonded emotionally with his unaffectionate parents. His unconscious pursuit of the emotional goal, combined with the addictive drug of pornography was his path to meet his emotional need. I also pointed out to him that the very existence of this type of pornography proved there was a market for it. That thought never crossed his mind.

All of the above examples are extreme, but I wanted to use extreme examples to create a stark contrast between very good emotional goals and how non-RHWR paths can be to achieve these emotional goals. To help all of us grow, it should be obvious that we need to differentiate between the goals and the paths we take to achieve those goals. The key to learning is repetition: everything we do is an attempt to meet an emotional goal; the emotional goal is good, the paths we take to achieve that goal need to be run through the grid of RHWR. Framed this way, this is what you must do:

1. List the non-RHWR behaviors you want to change.
2. Name the emotional goal(s) you are trying to achieve by that behavior (path).
3. List several RHWR paths (behaviors) you can choose to accomplish the same goal.
4. Name the emotional reward you will lose by switching paths. Grieve the loss, agree with the loss, and accept the loss.
5. Fight, fail, recover, and succeed in adopting other RHWR paths. "For a righteous man may fall seven times and rise again, but the wicked shall fall by calamity." (Proverbs 24:16)[2]

---

[2] The Holy Bible, New King James Version, Copyright © 1982 Thomas Nelson.

Chapter 2
The Blind Can't See

The Status Quo, Part II

Let's evaluate our individual status quo. The definition of the status quo is the way "things" currently are, and when applying it to ourselves, can be stated as "we are who we are." Holistically, who we are is our identity. In chapter four, we will delve deeper into this, but for our present purpose, I will focus on describing it as our current opinions, preferences, wants, desires, values, convictions, philosophy, and beliefs. These all exist within our unconscious and subconscious and become visible in our environment in the form of behavioral and emotional expressions. These expressions are proactive and reactive. They are proactive in our active pursuit of better micro (here-and-now) emotional experiences and in active pursuit of a better macro (quality of life and standard of living) experience. Our emotions become reactive when we feel as if something within our environment is hindering the proactive pursuit process. Our response tends to be to remove the obstacle. The goal is to simplify complex concepts first and then gradually dive into each part to explain the deeper ideas within.

Our Mental Model

Our mental model encapsulates all the elements above. Our mental model is the organic (ever-changing) product of 1) all the stored information we have in our brains and 2) the formulas we use to process that information. Our DNA, life experiences, and choices form our formulas. The DNA dictates everything physical about us. Within our DNA are the foundational formulas for our IQ, outward appearance, medical elements (like Autism or biologically caused disorders), as well as our personality/temperament. Besides the formation of our bodies, our gender also impacts the formulas of thinking in our brains. If the latter is a surprise to you, there are multiple books you can read on that topic, and I encourage you to do so. The key here is to understand that our DNA gives us "factory-installed" formulas that respond differently to our environment from birth.

As we execute our proactive and reactive response formulas, we store the results of each experience and deem them either good or bad, successful or unsuccessful, neutral, confusing or troubling, or a mixture of all of the above. Our life experiences impact, mold, and change how we see the world, view ourselves, and pursue our goals. Our DNA and life experiences create our unconscious and subconscious mental model, containing all the information/data gathered up to this point, along with the most current formulas we use to process, interpret, and evaluate each moment combined with the status quo of our quality of life, the world, and the meaning of ourselves in the world.

The final component that regularly morphs our formulas is choice. As we experience each situation in real-time, our mental model is hard at work assessing all the variables of each situation. While we may possess some experiential data on most of the variables and elements of each situation, we still must make a choice. Even no choice is still a choice. Our choices are the variable in each situation. Like a mysterious stranger, it is *the cumulative meaning behind the time stamp of the moment*. Please take a moment to fully take in what I'm trying to say in that sentence; it's important. Our conscious mind is the manager of choice, evaluating all the information, interpretations, and intensity (later, we'll get deeper into I^3) from our hard drive (conscious/subconscious). In addition to incorporating all the variables of this present moment, our conscious mind is creating a brand-new formula with the life span of a single breath. Every moment is unique, and the exact variables used in that formula never repeat. Our conscious mind is always calculating the most effective response to each situation. We choose in that moment, looking directly at our micro emotional goal, with our macro emotional goal always in our periphery. For example, we make immediate micro-goal decisions at work to be successful, determining what the most effective choices/responses are, while having our macro-goal of increasing our standard of living as another goal (trying to get a raise/promotion, etc.) We make a choice and experience the results of that choice, good or bad, and that data is stored in our mental model for future calculations. It may seem as if the process is solid and should result in a higher success rate, but alas, it does not (or else you wouldn't be reading this book). What is the issue then? The most obvious answer is that at any one moment, we lack all the information or the correct information to make the best decision. Secondly, our interpretation formulas can be way off, producing a wrong response decision. Thirdly, we do not incorporate all the variables of the situation or put too much or too little emphasis on each variable. Considering these things, the potential for mistakes is high. The question is not why the mental model process doesn't work; it is how it works correctly at all! Long ago, I determined that my mental model was faulty and learned not to trust it. Surprisingly, some of us may have way too much faith and trust in our mental models and dismiss any thought that our current way of thinking may be flawed. We are always seeking and exploring new information, which is great. However, new information and insights combined with inaccurate formulas (ways of using that information in decision-making) will still produce a poor product. Some of us run, avoid, ignore, or even suppress the negative emotions because we just don't want to face the fact that our thinking is way off. Even if we know it internally, we don't want to own it, and we get defensive if someone points it out. Let's address these issues.

Should Be or Not Should Be, that is the Question

As you can easily see, the process of our mental model is incredibly organic in nature, constantly changing and morphing. The growth and development of our way of thinking happens naturally and automatically throughout our lives, which is both passive (and active) in nature. The passive process occurs in our sub-conscious and the unconscious (DNA/previous life experiences), while the active process occurs in the conscious (free will). The most effective approach is to actively assess and evaluate the status quo in these areas, identifying necessary changes for greater success. While this seems obvious, many people impulsively accept their mental model's suggestions without questioning their validity. I named my business "Becoming More" because my goal is to equip people in the ongoing process (hence the participle, continuing and ongoing, form of "become") to become as successful as they can be. Success can be a desire to alleviate the current negative emotions that have become an impediment to their everyday life experience (by means of counseling), or they are doing well and want to become *more* successful and *more* effective in their role as a leader, parent, spouse, God-follower, etc. My tag line is: *Everyone becomes what they want to, only some people think about becoming more.* The "want" is defined as blindly accepting the suggestions of your mental model without challenge. Because your mental model suggests it, you naturally want to trust it. If your mental model suggests you hit the snooze button several times in the morning, order another drink at the bar, or tell your boss exactly what you think of him/her, that is what you *want* to do. Every human being does this, but some of us pause, evaluate what our mental model is proposing, and say in their conscious mind, "Wait, that is really dumb." The pause starts the process of re-programming our mental model to become *more* effective and successful. This is not just a mechanical process of think, feel, and do, trying to achieve micro and macro emotional goals. It is also a deeper evaluation of our *beliefs, opinions, convictions, values, and overall philosophy of life.* Where did you get those elements? Is it just a subjective choice related to our macro emotional goals or is there objective truth that informs us of what *should* be? If you have already bought into the RHWR concept, then you already believe in objective truth.

Born in China in 400 B.C

From childhood through my early adult years, I remember pondering about people around the world, such as the tribes in Africa and South America, Latin music, Hassidic Jews, Rap music, and NASCAR fans. Why are they like that? Why don't we do that? Are they weird or am I weird? Which one is right? And if it's not an issue of right or wrong, is one *better* than the other? What philosophy of life may have more wisdom? I applied these questions to the concept of the mental model. Since our DNA is so pivotal in creating our uniqueness, have you ever considered what it would be like if we had been born with a different personality and how we may think differently if we thought more like the opposite gender? Additionally, we regularly process how our lives would be different if we made different choices. Finally, we all have thought through how different we would be if our parents raised us in a better or worse way; or what we would be like if certain experiences would not have happened (like trauma); or if certain experiences had happened that didn't, like Uncle Rico's contemplation of how different his life would be if his team "would have taken state" (*Napolean Dynamite*). I'd like to take you on a radically different thought about how different we would be if we had a distinctly different life experience. How different would I be if I was born in China in 400 B.C., for example? If my personality and gender were the same, how different would my mental model be if I were raised in China during this period? This place and time are irrelevant. I honestly have no idea how different I would be. My goal is to attempt to answer my lifelong questions and come up with principles of wisdom I can use for myself and teach others. Two philosophical questions arise:

1. What beliefs, values, and opinions of my current mental model are because *I chose* them?
2. What parts and pieces of my current mental model are only a result of me being molded by my culture?

Besides China in 400 B.C., think through multiple examples using the categories of global, periodical, and cultural. Place yourself in any country, at any point in history, growing up in a particular culture, and ask yourself if you would have adopted the values, beliefs, and opinions of that culture or would you have rejected them. The chances are high that you and I would have adopted and thought just as those around us. On the other hand, in every culture, there are always those who associate with the counterculture and think differently. However, thinking similarly or differently than the greater culture could be a good thing or a bad thing, wise or unwise, right or wrong. If you were born in Germany in 1920, would you have supported the Nazis or rebelled against them? If you grew up in Afghanistan as a male, would you be a member of the Taliban? If you were in a white family in the southern states in the 1700s or 1800s, would you be a slave owner? Would you have been a part of the culture or fought against it? *All* of us would love to believe we would not participate in these atrocious mindsets, but do you also understand that the chances would be very high that you would have gone right along with it? Isn't that scary?

I am bewildered by the lack of critical thought among many in our culture who scoff at the forefathers of our country, deriding them because they were slaveowners. If we were born and raised in the families of our forefathers, I undoubtedly believe we would have mindlessly accepted it. Why do I say that? Because even today, there are those mindlessly accepting what our culture is telling them, touting the evil of the founders of our country and shaking their fists at their wickedness. Their issue isn't that they are disgusted that our forefathers were slaveowners; we all are. Their issue is their degree of disgust and derision, which involves declaring that they are more moral and righteous than the founders of our country. The other issue is their blindness to the concept of how much our childhood and culture impacts our philosophy of life. I can face the fact that if I grew up in any of the cultures above, there is a chance I would have, sadly, participated in those horrors. None of us really know what we would have done. The overall point I am trying to make, and will continue to make, is to not impulsively validate the product of our mental models, which includes our values, convictions, beliefs, and philosophy of life.

As I think through a variety of examples of global, periodic, and cultural situations, I consider the truth that every culture has strengths and weaknesses, rights and wrongs, and wisdom and foolishness. I compile the wisdom and insights from their philosophy of life to shape my worldview today. I am deeply disturbed by the horrors that humanity has committed and is committing. *I also am saddened by the historical truth that every great empire falls from within because of its decadence and immorality.* Do any of us really believe that America is exempt? Do any of us really believe that the evil in our country was greater at the time of its foundation than now? If we grew up 50, 100, or 200 years from now and looked back, what will be obvious to us about our current culture? I think, in many ways, we would look back and be shocked at the foolishness of what our current culture is promoting. Logic and truth have left most discussions in our cultural debate.

Why Our Culture Fails

Mental Model Formula Formation: *Grace and empathy without truth and boundaries is enablement. Truth and boundaries without grace and empathy are toxic.*

Throughout history, cultures swing back and forth like a pendulum when it comes to values and ideology. Our culture, for a time, pushed discipline and accountability to an extreme, which became toxic. Now the pendulum has certainly swung in the opposite direction and has hopefully reached the apex. Over-emphasizing empathy has become a severe problem at the societal and cultural levels in our current world. In all honesty, our culture has been shifting for decades and our society has now become the great defender of empathy while lacking any accountability in choosing paths that are not rational, healthy, wise, or right. We are in an epidemic of the end justifying the means. Many believe we are exercising empathy, sympathy, and love when we validate a person's pursuit of their emotional goal and then accept, validate, encourage, and applaud any path they want to achieve that emotional goal. If anyone attempts to suggest that their pathway does not pass the RHWR test, *they immediately assume that person is vehemently against that individual achieving their emotional goal.* The mere suggestion is viewed as appalling and abhorrent. This erroneous path suggests the one who challenges the path "hates" the one trying to achieve their emotional goal. The mere suggestion of an alternate path that may be more RHWR "triggers" an intense and highly emotional response. Ironically, the absolute truth is that those of us who do differentiate and challenge the non-RHWR path have MORE empathy, sympathy, and love for the individual than their advocates because we still philosophically submit our thinking to logic and truth. All to say, if the person continues on this path, the distance from point A to point B will become far greater and take much longer as they recover from the consequences of their non-RHWR path.

One final thought on this. The lack of reason and logic surrounding this discussion is so obvious, so extreme, that I step back and tell myself that there *must be* something else going on here. I believe there are other emotional goals at play other than the ones stated. What is the core issue? I believe it to be they have a different system of path evaluation. While most of humanity, throughout history, would use some grid like RHWR, our current society has adopted a different grid: individuality. Individuality becomes the ultimate emotional goal. *When this happens, the RHWR grid dissolves because it is paradoxical to apply a grid that is based on objective logic and truth to achieve an emotional goal that is purely subjective in nature.* There are those who say they are practicing empathy and sympathy, trying to help others achieve the goals of love and identity, but their rationale has a record-setting low *face validity* (face validity is a research term that measures how well a test truly measures what it purports to measure). It is a test to measure how the external represents the reality of the internal. The reality of the internal in this current discussion doesn't, at its core, have to do with all those beautiful principles of empathy, sympathy, love, and identity. Why? Because, like every other path throughout history, people who truly have empathy, sympathy, love, and identity bring logic and truth to the discussion. If they were to change their message to have high face validity, instead of saying they are promoting love and empathy, they would have to admit their true goals are actually individuality and autonomy. Autonomy comes from two Greek words "autos" (self) and "nomos" (law) . . . self-law. Let me state very clearly that there are an endless number of areas of our lives where individuality and autonomy are beautiful and bring out the best creativity and ingenuity within humanity. But in each of these areas, all paths pass the RHWR grid with flying colors! The issue, again, is that some paths don't pass the RHWR test, which in turn causes harm to both them and others. It is apparent to most of the population because of the irrational and illogical omission of truth. When we present these ideas based on reason, logic, and truth and discuss what RHWR is, we still meet opposition. If logic and truth have left the discussion, then how can there be any solution? Individuality and autonomy are the masters behind the scenes, presenting themselves as love and empathy, which results in the path and goal becoming enmeshed and indistinguishable. The *only* way we will see a reversal in this ideology comes when we begin to experience the painful ramifications of this logic-less and truth-less cultural experience. Hence, *grace and empathy without truth and boundaries are enablement.*

    I intentionally did not mention any specific examples above for very strategic reasons. I have found when people propose a general point and are asked to provide proof, examples are given. In turn, the examples themselves become the focus and are picked apart while the original point gets completely lost. Furthermore, my goal is to keep the theory of emotional goal/RHWR path at the forefront to teach and equip you, the reader, with the theory. In addition, I tried to illustrate examples that most would agree are detrimental paths (alcohol use, sexual behaviors, and cutting) and emphasize the consequences. Likewise, many counselors fall short of fulfilling their calling because they simply practice the skill of empathy, helping the client feel heard and accepted, but sadly the client never truly changes at the core level. For those of you who are committed to true growth and development, my hope is that I have achieved the emotional goal of peace and clarity for you. It makes sense to understand why you believe the way you believe. Suppose you find yourself feeling angry right now and are debating whether to continue reading. May I point out that you were most likely "nodding" in the original examples (alcohol, adultery, and cutting), but now you find yourself dismissing the theory. May I simply ask you what are you afraid of? What bad happens if this is true? What emotional goal of yours is being blocked right now? Can you be open to the possibility you may be a bit blind in your thinking strategies and possibly missing something right now? Our ability to truly grow, at the soul level, is inextricably linked to our ability to understand we are accountable to what is RHWR. We must absolutely own what we need to own and be open to the fact that we possess blind spots in our lives and need a system of critical thinking to improve everyone's quality of life.

Our mental models need a tune-up. We should look objectively at our mental model and be honest with ourselves, realizing we are guilty sometimes of blindly adopting the values, beliefs, and opinions of our greater culture. At any point in history and life, there is a RHWR way to think and a non-RHWR way to think. We need more information, better information, and *true* information in our hard drives. With improved information downloaded into our hard drives, we can transform the formulas used to produce improved conclusions, opinions, and decisions that are RHWR. We also need to switch the object of focus when we experience negative emotions from outside to inside.

I am trying to 1) teach you why we are the way we are, 2) convince you, the reader, why we need to challenge the way we think, which is the only way to 3) be able to have the strength to face the deepest of our negative emotions to find the richness of peace and rest in our souls. At this point, it should be obvious we all need to have enough skepticism about the validity of what our mental models produce. Having this skepticism will automatically result in a lower level of emotional intensity, because we are not as dogmatically confident in our opinion that we are right and anyone who opposes is wrong and offensive.

Back to the Surface: What Should Be and What Should Not Be

Is there some area of your life that you find troublesome and want to change, *or* is your interpretation of this aspect incorrect, and you should be content, even grateful, for this area of your life? For example, I have some physical features that I have assessed as undesirable. The contrast between my physical features and my wife's is stark. Whenever we take a selfie, my first impression is that we are the real-life version of Quasimodo and Esmerelda. Have you ever seen a couple and thought to yourself, "He must either be rich or have a great personality?" That would be your initial reaction if you saw a picture of us. I have some physical features I wish were different, but I can't change many of them, so what needs to change is my interpretation of these features. If I change how I view my physical features that I can't change, then my emotions change. By the way, my wife loves my personality.

However, my current health and weight may *actually* need to change to a healthier status. But if I don't like the fact that my hair is thinning, should I pursue excessive "lengths" to find a way to thicken my hair or be content with the status quo, interpreting it as a simple process of aging and accept it? I absolutely don't begrudge those who change aspects of their physical features (hair transplants, tummy tucks, etc.). My point is that some of us just may need to change our interpretation, that's all. What if our opinion of the status quo doesn't need to change, but there are others in our life who do believe some component of our status quo needs to change? Do we automatically agree, or do we automatically dismiss and ignore? If we are to be totally honest, there are areas of our lives that we don't think should change but, in all reality, they should, (such as some of our personal habits). Wait. Who determined it should change? Why do I have to be the one to change? If their opinion is wrong, they are the one who needs to change, right?

In my own reflections on my work with thousands of individuals, the measurement of my success is more than equipping them to get from point A to point B. I must help them process the underlying concepts of "what is" versus "what should be" and how they both were created in the first place. Before evaluating yourself, look at people in your own life. It's easier to look objectively at others for objective truth because we can be defensive about our own weaknesses, failings, etc. If we pull ourselves out of the topic/concept for a minute and instead of trying to apply the principle to ourselves, which may produce negative emotions, we should step back, be objective, and apply the principle to other people first, so we can more quickly arrive at wisdom and truth, and then apply it to ourselves.

Bless Their Heart

Have you ever had the following thought about another human being, "Wow, they don't get it. They are so defensive and don't even realize it hurts both them and others around them. They are so blind"? I spent most of my life in Michigan and always loved hearing about Southern hospitality. So, when I moved to Texas, I experienced that genuine Southern hospitality firsthand. I found that Southerners have much in common with our kin in England because they both are known to have a tongue-in-cheek approach to relationships. "Bless your heart" is a common saying here and disguised as a form of Southern hospitality. In reality, it is a back-handed way of saying, "You're clueless and just don't get it, honey." We can probably name someone like this and honestly know we are right, and they are wrong (if they disagree) or are blind (if they don't even see it). Sometimes it is a combination. Some people acknowledge the validity of a particular behavior needing to be on the list but are completely blind as to the degree of the issue. They say, "Yeah, I know I need to work on that", and we say to ourselves, "But you have no clue how bad it is." Despite agreeing with the item, there is no real effort or urgency in addressing it.

Now, bring it back into the subjective realm and *be open to the idea that you may come to someone's mind if they were asked to think of someone who doesn't "get it."* Hopefully, at this point it is apparent that we need help from others to fully gain insight into what we need to change and how important it is that we do change.

The Johari Window and the Eradication of the Blind Area

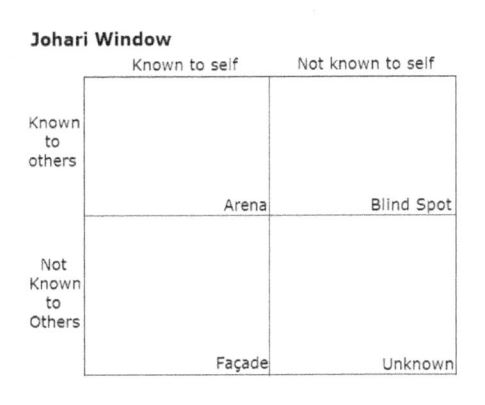

Johari Window

	Known to self	Not known to self
Known to others	Arena	Blind Spot
Not Known to Others	Façade	Unknown

Like the principle of organizational change discussed in Chapter One, I was exposed early in my life to the Johari Window Model. The Johari Window Model is a technique produced by two psychologists Joseph Luft and Harrington Ingham (Joe and Harry, combined to become Johari) in 1955. The overall goal is to help people have a better understanding of themselves and their relationships. It is described as a window because there are four boxes joined together to form a "window". The four windows are labeled Arena/Open, Façade/Hidden, Blind, and Unknown.

Information that is easily known to other people and known to self is the Arena/Open area. I've already disclosed to you that I was a pastor, counselor, coach and consultant, and professor. That is my "open" information that you know, and I know. Then there is information about myself that is known to me, but not known to you. That is the Façade/Closed area. This means there is information that I want to remain hidden and unknown to the world. We all have a closed area containing many truths and facts about our lives. Why? Because we are fearful. We are all scared. If other people knew that information about us, we believe they would think less of us and possibly tell other people, which would influence other people to think less about us. This is why it is called the Façade area, because we create a façade when we are trying to influence what other people think about us by withholding certain information from them. We all choose what information we are willing to move from the Closed area to the Open area and to whom we reveal this information.

Going Deeper into the Closed Area (Foreshadowing of a Source of Negative Emotions)

You will notice a consistent practice I use throughout this book. Whenever a concept is discussed that refers to a human being resisting in some way, shape, or form doing something that is good and healthy, I want to step back and examine what the motivation or goal may be and when or why we choose to do that. Yes, revealing information in the Closed area would expose information that others could use against us and hurt us. What bad happens if we did reveal information in the Closed area? But what bad happens if this information is not revealed? What good happens if this information is revealed? What good happens if this information is not revealed? Each piece of information will produce different answers. If we truly have the desire to grow, mature, and improve who we are at the deepest level of our souls, there is some information that we absolutely need to reveal.

Even though we know this to be true, we still hesitate to share this information out of the fear that it may damage some relationships in our lives. To illustrate, I'll use one of the best verses that describe who Jesus Christ is and how He interacts with all of us. You will notice the same words from the formula formation principle above. John 1:14 states, "The Word became flesh and made his dwelling among us. We have seen his glory, the glory of the one and only Son, who came from the Father, *full of grace and truth.*" The last phrase is the focus of my point. Throughout the gospels, when we read about each interaction Jesus had with people, His statements were graceful and empathic. He spoke the truth, addressing where people were wrong and needed to change. Anyone who reads the gospels can't walk away and criticize Jesus's approach to people. He achieved both goals (grace and truth) with each individual/group. The only people He gave truth to, with a great deal of intensity, were the people who wouldn't admit they were blind, refused to own anything, and were opposed to being open to correction. Interesting.

Describing Jesus, or God, as full of grace and truth is a theological and philosophical concept that is far-reaching and has great depths of knowledge, insight, and understanding that can never be fully understood as far as its impact and meaning. But if we keep it on the surface and apply it to interpersonal relationships, it becomes an extremely effective principle. As I (just like you) form relationships, I share general information about myself. When that information is received positively (with empathy and grace), I feel safe with that person and confident to share more truth about myself. Relationships grow and deepen if grace is received each time more truth is revealed. At some point in the relationship, permission to speak the truth is either asked for and/or granted because enough grace has been experienced, achieving emotional safety. Thus, more truth is comfortably shared. A critical realization test for us is when we share the truth about ourselves, and we are judged, void of grace. At that point, the sharing of further information on a deeper level ceases and becomes officially locked within the Closed Area of the Johari Window because we no longer feel safe. Think of your closest relationships and evaluate why you haven't shared with them more details about yourself. It very well may be because you are convinced, correctly or incorrectly, that you won't receive grace from them. When someone knows something about us that we wish wasn't true and lacks grace and empathy, it feels toxic.

Today, we see how the push for tolerance, under the guise of empathy, has been exaggerated to an extreme. Don't misunderstand—empathy is essential when balanced with grace and truth, but anything taken to an extreme becomes a weakness. I believe many now err on the side of empathy and sympathy to avoid being labeled "toxic". In addition, many may be motivated by their own desire to avoid negative emotions and the desire of acceptance over the necessities of truth and boundaries on behaviors. The result is irresponsible enablement. Wisdom dictates that in every relationship, both goals need to be always achieved. I often advise clients when they need to be truthful with a loved one in their life, they make a statement of grace, love, and empathy, such as "I love you and am committed to you." Then, they share the truth, "What you are doing is not RHWR, and you need to really consider changing." Then followed by another statement of grace, "I am for you and committed to you. I love you."

The Hidden and Blind Areas of the Johari Window

The area that is not known to you or me is the Hidden area. Here are the aspects about myself that I don't even know and, of course, if I don't know them, neither do you. It's simply hidden, and shedding light on this area is often a lifelong process of growth and discovery. It involves the deepest of self-reflections and obtaining the most profound of insights. Here we basically find our meaning, our identity, our purpose, etc. I hope that by reading this book, the journey becomes more tangible so that you can become more strategic in achieving the macro goal of increasing your quality of life.

The final area, the area that has caused me the greatest amount of consternation, fear, and trepidation, is the fourth area of the Johari Window, called the Blind area. The Blind area is the area that I don't see about myself, *but you do*. Just the thought alone that other people see things about me that I don't see about myself gives me a reason to pause. On the flip side, there are certainly areas, aspects, details of my life, my personality, my gifts, skills, and abilities that others see that I don't that can be *positive*. Most of us are critical of ourselves, underestimate our own value, and need others to give us these objective truths so that we can be more successful. When it comes to areas of my life that are positive and encouraging, I want to be aware of those areas and readily accept those items that are positive and encouraging as objective truth.

The greater endeavor, of course, is to unveil the areas that we don't see about ourselves that others see as negative. I have already encouraged you to think of people throughout your life who may have a blind area you desperately wish they would see. So, doesn't it logically stand to reason that you may possess areas of your life that you may be unaware of, and others may greatly wish you could see? The only way for you to avoid being the "their" in "bless their heart" is if someone chooses to be brave and share with you the truth. But wouldn't doing so risk the relationship? My question is: if it is indeed your issue and not theirs, why would they struggle to tell you? Your blindness is your issue, especially if it's causing others pain. It's not their responsibility to tell you, it's your responsibility to inquire what it may be. It is each of our responsibilities to grow and mature in order to add value to other's lives. Having negative traits that hurt others or create a negative atmosphere is not the other's responsibility to deal with; it is our job to objectively evaluate it and ask ourselves if we see traits in others that need to change. We often believe that when someone gets up the nerve to confront us about an offensive aspect of our personality, we feel they are the only person who feels that way. There is one way to find out: proactively ask other people in your life if they feel the same way. Don't assume it's just that one person's issue. Do you think there might be a gap between your subjective view of yourself and the objective view of yourself that others hold? How are you going to close that gap?

The Beginning of the Objective/Subjective Process of View of Self

My work, whether as a pastor, counselor, director, professor, coach, or consultant, has focused on guiding others to prioritize objective truth over subjective experience and eliminate blind spots. Objective truth comes from external sources: our parents, our family, our friends, society, culture, and the like. In addition, and most importantly, objective truth comes from God. What every religion has in common are commitments to morality, selflessness, and the pursuit of wisdom. Anyone or anything that has influence in our lives suggests items they believe should be included in our personal growth and development plan (our point B). We first determine whether we agree to adopt that opinion or dismiss it. If we agree with it, adding it to our list only creates more distance from point A to point B. Even if we disagree with it, we will experience tension because of the paradox between what is and what should be. We burn copious amounts of emotional energy trying to reconcile the disconnect between what others believe about us and what we believe about ourselves. Even if we agree, we are not nearly as motivated to do those things because they aren't produced from within us. However, you now know that there are new areas in your personal development plan (point B) that you must incorporate outside of yourself because it is true, and it is objective. Though it can be painful, you must create a strategy to turn unreached goals into a new status quo, making them a true part of who you are. To be sure, don't think that the two lists in point B are entirely separate because many of the items do overlap. Many suggestions we receive from the objective sources (others) and objective truth (the Lord), were already in either the Open or Closed areas of our Johari Window. It is only those items that are in the Blind area that you must figure out your strategy for uncovering them and moving them into the light. As illustrated in the section on the mental model, we must be in a constant search for that objective truth. All of us have experienced objective opinions that do not align with objective truth, which makes us cautious when we hear those objective opinions. However, we must be just as cautious when we receive subjective opinions from our mental models.

Societal Objective Truth

I think we can all agree on the need for laws in our society, otherwise it would be anarchy. We understand that these laws are necessary because disobeying them would harm others, as well as ourselves. Have you considered the fact that every law in society has some tie to morality? There isn't one law in society, not one, that doesn't have morality attached to it. I remember sitting in my government class in 9th grade, and the topic was the Prohibition Era in America. My teacher asked us at the conclusion of the discussion: what the ultimate reason was for Prohibition's failure? He proceeded to answer his own question, "Because you can't make laws against people's morals." Something in me sprung up, and I immediately raised my hand (I didn't give him an opportunity to call on me) and proclaimed, "What law exists that is not based on morals?" He didn't respond. Every law rooted in morality, where individuality is secondary to protecting the rights of others first and then themselves. Even speed limits are set because objective truth states that if the primary emotional goal in determining driving laws were individuality and autonomy--driven (excuse the pun), the consequences would be catastrophic, right? I am absolutely pounding the point that the only way to have a successful society is for all of us to submit ourselves to objective truth standards like RHWR, not only on a macro, societal level, but all the way down to our micro, personal level in the formation of who we are as people.

Equipping: Using the Concept of Objective Truth in Parenting

To illustrate the contrast between the subjective and objective view of self, allow me to use an illustration from marriage counseling and parenting. As parents, we strive to raise great kids, and, as all parents know, it is sometimes a very arduous process. Why is it sometimes so difficult? The degree of difficulty is directly correlated to how much our child disagrees with our opinion of where they need to grow, right? Why would they disagree with us? Well, from infancy, we are born with a tenacious drive to improve our quality of life using the path of our choice to achieve that goal. This process continues throughout childhood and into our teenage years. We try to coach our children to understand the difference between their subjective view of themselves to more of an objective view. It's a never-ending process of helping our young ones evaluate their paths through the objective RHWR grid (or some form of it). Our children, like us, fight against the application of this grid because all of us are committed to what we *want* to do. When our children inevitably learn the skill to objectively evaluate us humans that also need to grow, the resistance to objective RHWR only grows. It is human nature to evaluate the evaluator. You may have heard the saying, "You can't separate the message from the messenger." It is better interpreted as whenever a person suggests you need to change; you automatically start scanning them for hypocrisy. With our children, this happens in three ways: First, children also have their own opinions on our own point A and what our point B should be and they want to know what is taking us so long to get to our point B. Secondly, they get upset or frustrated because we disagree with them on what *our* point B should be. And finally, they struggle with losing respect for us if we are blind to our point B, invoke a double standard, or our urgency to change is too low. If we want our children to transition from subjective to objective, we must model it for them. We must hold them accountable to live morally and uphold strong principles. But additionally, we need to be humble, own our mistakes, and show them how to recover from failure because we know it is easy for our children to feel like they are constantly failing. Conversely, lacking humility discredits us, and we lose their respect. Show them how to be teachable and teach them how to fail, as well as how to recover and grow. Show them how to achieve both goals of grace and truth with yourselves and with them. If we want them to be accountable to objective truth (RHWR), then we need to model it for them. Our children need to feel that we are not forcing them into a mold of our own making. I encourage parents to show their children that the goals for our parenting are objective and ubiquitous (present for everyone). Successful parenting is defined by our children becoming independent, successful, mature adults. Say to them,

> "I am not imposing my ideals and values on you; my goal is to equip you and coach you to become an independent, successful, mature adult. Think of it like this, on one end is the 25-year-old (child's name) who is independent, successful, and mature, and on the other end is you at your current age. There is a gap between you right now and you at 25. This is not a conversation between you and me, but between the present-day you and you as an independent, successful, mature adult. When you are 25, you will look back at your current age and have the *exact same advice* that I am giving to you right now. I love you, and I want to equip and coach you to become that

person." In addition, I would say, "Where I am selfish in this process is I am doing everything I can to make sure your future college roommate and spouse don't disparage me over the fact that they are having to deal with your lack of independence, lack of success, and immaturity, so let's keep working".

Kids need a strong investment in coaching from their parents to help them become the best version of themselves. Parental coaching does not shy away from correction, realizes the power of encouragement, and continually equips them for the real world. The countless number of parents I have presented this mindset to feel a great sense of relief because it eliminates the "fight" that the child perceives as parents imposing their own "opinions" on them. Like RHWR, there is objective truth among all humanity when we say that our children should be independent, successful, and mature. Every parent everywhere, at any point in history, agrees with that. Applying this process is rhetorical, it's common sense, it's ubiquitous, it transcends all cultures, all nations, all times…to train our children to be independent, successful, and mature. Objective truth hovers above us all, and our individual point B's and paths don't only impact us personally but also the lives of others. There must be rules, boundaries and standards by which all humans align themselves, despite any frustration it may cause as it may appear to block their main emotional goal of individuality and autonomy.

It is also important to teach our children to incorporate objective values, such as selflessness. Children don't naturally recognize the long-term effects of their obsession with individuality and autonomy. Pursuing these emotional goals creates the greatest emotional reward for them, but if this process becomes cemented, they will be extremely weak in their emotional intelligence skills of impulse control and delay of gratification. This can absolutely ruin their chances of success in life and relationships. Another principle I give to parents, in addition to raising our children to be independent, successful, and mature, is the principle of "duty and discipline before dopamine." As adults, we do this every single day. Any independent, successful, and mature adult practices this principle. We work before we play. We do our household responsibilities before we relax. We eat vegetables before ice cream. It's standard, or it should be. Adults come to me for counseling, wanting to be better equipped to apply this principle. They recognize they are suffering the consequences of not mastering this principle, mainly because many of their parents did not fulfill the goal of truth and boundaries, but emphasized the goal of grace and empathy, leading to their enablement. As stated earlier, grace and empathy without truth and boundaries is enablement. Both goals need to be achieved. As adults, they suffer from low impulse control and find themselves constantly choosing the wrong RHWR path to achieve their emotional goals. We need to train our children in these principles so that they may have hope for a future of personal and relational success. The resistance we may experience from our children is understandably rooted in their quest of the reward and immediate emotional goal being met. Yet their shortsightedness prevents them from seeing the future unintended consequences of either choosing their immediate emotional goals or non-RHWR paths.

Not Just Openness to, but Obsession with, Objective Truth

There are a copious number of Scriptures, along with John 1:14 (Jesus came full of grace and truth), that have been foundational in forming the basic theories in my career. In Proverbs, it states that the goal is to search for wisdom, knowledge and understanding as if it is literally hidden treasure. Proverbs 2:1-11 states:

My son, if you accept my words
    and store up my commands within you,
2 turning your ear to wisdom
    and applying your heart to understanding—
3 indeed, if you call out for insight
    and cry aloud for understanding,
4 and if you look for it as for silver
    and search for it as for hidden treasure,
5 then you will understand the fear of the Lord
    and find the knowledge of God.
6 For the Lord gives wisdom;
    from his mouth come knowledge and understanding.
7 He holds success in store for the upright,
    he is a shield to those whose walk is blameless,
8 for he guards the course of the just
    and protects the way of his faithful ones.
9 Then you will understand what is right and just
    and fair—every good path.
10 For wisdom will enter your heart,
    and knowledge will be pleasant to your soul.
11 Discretion will protect you,
    and understanding will guard you.

There are several points I want to make. First, if you must search for something, you have yet to find it and, therefore, do not possess it. Secondly, notice the intensity and desperation by which we are to search for knowledge, insight, wisdom, and understanding. We "turn our ear to it," meaning we are open to it. Next, it states we are to "call out for it" and "cry aloud for it" and to "search for it as if it were a hidden treasure." Think of all the things in life right now you are the most desperate to obtain. We cry out for a solution to our finances, to the pain in our marriage, the suffering of being under a poor leader at work, etc., but we should also be crying out for insight, wisdom, and understanding. To summarize a major proposition of this book, we must first understand how we may be blind in many areas, grasp the fact that our mental models produce suggestions and conclusions that should be evaluated, and seek insight and wisdom revealing to us exactly the areas we are blind. These safeguards will help improve our thinking "formulas" and equip us with more effective responses.

Be warned that the information we discover in wisdom, knowledge, and understanding, we may not initially agree with and want to reject. Therein lies the battle of humanity because the truths in wisdom, knowledge and understanding are often found in our blind areas and difficult to obtain. And quite honestly, incorporating those truths and processes can be painful. Unfortunately, we all know relationships where the refusal of, agreement with, and adoption of these objective truths is lifelong and, even more sadly, has yet to be achieved. I do find many people open and desirous of this type of insight; however, many fail to follow through with the intensity required to discover this insight by exposing themselves emotionally to apply the necessary insights.

Equipping: The Habit of Proactive Teachability

Teachability can, in many ways, be likened to humility, which is considering other people over yourself. I promote using the word "teachability" over the word "humility" because some misinterpret the term by believing it is the practice of diminishing their value and worth. Humility is a complex heart issue. Conversely, teachability is simply an attribute that means we know we don't know everything and are open to learning from others. Teachability and humility are the opposite of pride. What is the practical definition of pride? Pride is a dismissive response to environmental opinions. Pride is when the person concludes they already have all the information/data they need in their mental models. Not only that, but they also have the most effective formulas and critical thinking to automatically produce the right opinions and conclusions. Frankly put, they don't need your insight. To be fully transparent, I struggle to have patience with these people, but I must remember that I truly believe at the core of that mindset is a deep vacuum of value and worth. They default to an automatic pride response because it's too painful for them to go through the process of exposing these deep insecurities.

On the contrary, teachable people are open to and desirous of information that they don't possess, and secondly, they are open to and desirous of new ways of thinking and processing. When teachable people are presented with new information, they can now process it with a new formula or way of thinking or a new set of eyes that they didn't have before. Those of us who remember taking Algebra know that in a formula, if the x^2 should be an x^3, the product of the formula will be wrong. Just as in our mental model process, wrong formulas mean incorrect interpretations (biases, assumptions, etc.) of information presented to us.

Now let's combine the philosophy of Proverbs 2 with the concept of teachability. I would say most of us only practice *reactive* teachability. What does that mean? Reactive teachability is when someone builds up the courage to approach us to point out the fact that we are lacking information or, more difficult yet, have an incorrect way of thinking. They are nervous to start a conflict because addressing a legitimate issue may result in the person feeling unsafe or exposed. Some have no hesitancy in calling out blind spots, but most hesitate and avoid it out of fear of conflict. Either way, reactive teachability is when people come into our lives and tell us that we need to be corrected in some way, in a grace-and-truth way. Those who are truly teachable have no problem with that. In fact, we invite the insight because we're open to and desirous of that change. We understand that we may have blind areas and want them to eradicate them. Isn't that a healthy goal? So, ultimately, our maturity and teachability are essential in minimizing and shrinking the three areas of our closed, hidden, and blind boxes within the Johari Window. The result is an expansion of our open areas, leading to true life fulfillment.

We can never arrive at this fulfillment with reactive teachability alone. Why? Reactive teachability is rarely effective because everyone naturally resists these confrontations out of fear it will result in defensiveness or an attack. To be the most effective in eradicating the closed, hidden, and blind areas, we must do more than reactive teachability, hoping and waiting for others to build up the courage to come to us. To accomplish this, we must practice *proactive* teachability. It is the RHWR path of regularly going to people in your life and asking them the hard questions: "Where am I blind? How can I grow? How can I be better?" But even if we do this, some may still be hesitant to be completely honest out of the same fear of conflict; you must, therefore, "pull" it out of them. After asking these questions, follow up by saying, "I'm not looking for the obvious information, I want the information in the back of your mind that you would never share with me. That is the information I need for two reasons; first, I may be blind to that information and am desperate to gain insight, wisdom, knowledge, and understanding. The second reason is that you may have information or an opinion or conclusion about me that may be incorrect because of some misunderstanding or experience, and I would love the opportunity to correct that."

If you feel that this is too extreme, then what other paths can you come up with to get true feedback from others and fulfill the principle of Proverbs 2? Considering the application of this technique, is there anyone you know, perhaps even yourself, that *desperately* needs to practice proactive teachability? As a matter of fact, shouldn't every human being practice this? Imagine what our world would be like. Even if you don't receive any new information from the person, or the information they offer is faulty, think about the transformational impact on each of you through this exercise. What if you practiced this at work? What if you practiced this with your family?

I often ask my clients questions like, "Are you a good wife?" Are you a good husband?" Often their answers can be quite humorous. Without even thinking, they may reply, "Well, there are different areas I need to improve, but yeah, I think so." I would then ask, "Have you ever asked your wife if you're good husband?" or "Have you ever asked your husband if you're a good wife?" Who should have a major say in whether we are a good spouse? Then why haven't we asked them? Are you a good parent? Are you a good listener? Are you a good boss? Have you ever asked the people you are listening to if they feel heard by you? Have you ever asked your children how you can improve as a parent? (You may be surprised by their answers). Have you ever asked your followers if you are a good leader? There's no need to feel defensive as to why you haven't or wouldn't; just ask them. It's not as if they hold the monopoly on the objective truth in each of these respective roles, but they absolutely may have information about you that you don't possess about yourself (the good ole blind area). Remember, the bonus in doing this is also building relationships based on your humility, teachability, and transparency. These are incredibly powerful human traits people admire and have the impact of motivating and convicting others to do the same.

Summary

Our mental models are an accumulation of a vast amount of information we have gathered throughout our lives, including the numerous formulas we use in interpreting and responding to every situation. These formulas are created from our DNA, life experiences, and choices. As we live, our mental models constantly change as we gain information and learn how to be more successful in accomplishing our micro (here-and-now) and macro (quality of life/standard of living) emotional goals. However, our philosophy of life, comprised of our convictions, values, and beliefs about morality, also impacts and helps to form our quality of life. The admission that our mental model may be flawed in more ways than we may be aware of and may consist of numerous blind spots is essential to our mental health and relationships. As we apply the RHWR grid to the paths we use to achieve our micro and macro emotional goals, we must also do the same with our philosophy of life. The only way for this to be truly successful is to be obsessed with eradicating our blind areas and consumed with gaining more insight, wisdom, and understanding. If you are ready, let's open that door together and walk the path toward gaining insight, wisdom, and understanding, unlocking the power of our negative emotions.

Chapter 3
Our Emotional Storms

The Odd Counselor

One of my jobs involved working as an Organizational Development Strategist for an assessments company in Texas that had a system for benchmarking top performers, as well as a 360-degree tool for evaluating their managers' and leaders' ability to influence others in their organizations. I traveled the country working with senior leadership teams, helping them develop team synergy to execute their business strategy more effectively. Their ability to synergize as a team was directly correlated with their skills in emotional intelligence. Each of their leaders would then participate in an eight-week executive coaching process with me. I have taken a variety of career assessments throughout my life, and I don't remember my top matches, but one thing I do know was that a counselor was not one of them. I am a driven, gregarious extrovert, whereas the profile for a counselor would be more of an agreeable, detailed introvert. These aren't "laws" but more of a stereotypical fit based on the nature of the work. Here is the story of how I entered the field of psychology and counseling.

I became a Christian in Junior Church when I was just six or seven years old. This was at Lake Center Bible Church in Portage,

MI. Soon after, my parents quit going to church, which meant I quit going to church. They had just purchased an old farmhouse that needed to be completely renovated, so they spent evenings and weekends pouring into that. Without consistent Christian influence, I went through the party-hearty teenage years, and then suffered the consequences for those years, and then recommitted my life to Christ shortly before I turned 21. I started attending church again, visiting various churches, but eventually landing back at the same church I attended as a child. The same pastors and leaders of Junior Church were still there, and I just had the feeling of being "home". After a year or so of attending church, my love for the Lord grew greatly. I was working as a Produce Manager at the local grocery store at the time, and I remember being overwhelmed with my love for the Lord, thinking about it constantly. A deeper vision and purpose was welling up in me, and one day, while wrapping grapes in cellophane to display and sell, I suddenly put the package of grapes down on the wrapper, walked out, and stood in front of the produce case. I thought to myself, "All of this food will rot, but human souls will live forever." After work, I called the Associate Pastor, Gordon Daam, set up a meeting with him, and passionately expressed that I felt like I was being called into the ministry. We set up a time to meet with the Senior Pastor, Dr. Terry Puett, and they came up with the idea to send me on a short-term mission's trip to Guyana, South America. So, in 1993, I boarded my first ever flight and flew from Kalamazoo, MI, to Chicago, to Puerto Rico, to Trinidad and Tobago, and then on to Georgetown, Guyana. I literally had a boxed radiator for the missionary's truck as one of my suitcases and a carry-on filled with a water pump and Bible verse memory packs. I couldn't do that today! After spending ten weeks in Guyana, I knew my calling to the ministry was sure and came back, worked to pay off debt, and left the fall of 1994 for upstate New York to attend Word of Life Bible Institute for their one-year Bible training program. Thankfully, I was able to complete my summer ministry internship at my church during the following summer. By this time, the church had switched senior pastors, and after my internship, the new senior pastor offered me the position of Youth Pastor. I began my ministry in December of 1995. At that point, I wanted to go to seminary but had not yet completed my bachelor's degree. I attended Western Michigan University for three years after high school but then quit shortly after I recommitted my life to Christ. By the time I completed the one-year Bible institute, I had about 160 credits to my name but no degree. There were apparently enough people like me because in the mid-90's, colleges started creating adult and continuing education programs to help all of us complete our degrees. I enrolled at Cornerstone University in the spring, and the only degree they offered at the time for that program was a bachelor's in organizational leadership. It didn't matter to me because my focus was to get my degree so I could start seminary.

After finally graduating with my bachelor's degree, I enrolled in my first semester of seminary in the fall of 1997. I started with the core courses of the Master of Divinity degree program, one of which was philosophy of counseling. What I learned in that course became a watershed moment for me. My eyes opened to the insight and wisdom in the material, and how it would equip me to be a better pastor. In addition, the proverbial scales fell from my eyes when the professor was lecturing, and I felt like he was laying my soul wide open before me. It was at that moment that I met with my advisor and mapped out the process to earn a dual master's degree: a Master of

Divinity and a Master of Arts in Counseling. I completed my MDiv in three years and then graduated with my MA in Counseling three years later in 2003.

I believe my path to counseling was formed more by my circumstances than my natural temperament. I learned the theories and the skills of counseling, but my personality manifests itself in my theory of how to help clients change and achieve their goals. I tell clients that I am an "active" counselor, I don't just do "talk and listen" therapy. My goal is to equip clients to become very effective in their emotional management with actual skills and techniques. However, let me quickly give the disclaimer that I am completely sold on the person-centered skills of empathy, genuineness, and positive regard. I tell apprehensive clients that they are safe with me and that creating a trusting therapeutic relationship is mandatory for transparency and true change to take place. As stated in the last chapter, many counselors view empathy as the measurement of the success of therapy instead of seeing it as a foundational pre-requisite for change to take place.

The measurements of success for my counseling are one, the alleviation of the *severity* of the negative emotions (not the eradication of them). And two, equipping the client with the skills and techniques of emotional intelligence and critical thinking so they are more effective and *self-sufficient* in the process of emotional management. Another brand of counselors certainly help their clients with their emotional goals, but they don't equip the clients to become self-sufficient in this process, which then creates a dependency of the client on the counselor to solve their problems. I absolutely trust my colleague's intentions and true desire to help their clients. But like any field and any career, there is certainly a bell curve of skillset, proficiency, and effectiveness among all practitioners. The counselor I struggle with the most is the person who is motivated to become a counselor out of the desire to share congruency in woundedness. As I stated in my introduction, you can't impart what you don't possess. If you are not healed as a counselor, you certainly can't be effective in helping others heal. If we as therapists haven't walked into our own dark places and faced the deepest of negative emotions and owned our responsibility to manage our own negative emotions, we can by no means be successful at helping others do the same. Therapists are human too, and we all make mistakes, and we all experience the same emotional storms everyone else faces, but we are ethically obligated to heal and master the very process we are asking the client to walk through.

Two years after completing my Master of Arts in Counseling, I began pursuing my PhD in Counselor Education & Supervision with Regent University. Prior to that, I started working as an adjunct professor for my alma mater, Cornerstone University, teaching the same Organizational Leadership courses I took in my undergrad. The more I taught those courses, the more I fell in love with the material. Around the same time, I stumbled upon the book *Emotional Intelligence* by Daniel Goleman while on vacation. I was perusing the psychology section at Barnes and Noble and was intrigued by the title of the book. I was more intrigued by the subtitle, *Why it can matter more than IQ*. Reading that book became another defining moment for me, considering its viral application in so many areas. The title of my dissertation was *The Relationship of Emotional Intelligence with Job Satisfaction and Organizational Commitment*. After I graduated in 2008, I began to practice organizational consulting and executive coaching with a high-powered Fortune 500 medical device company and since then have coached hundreds of leaders. Even though the focus of my work with leaders is on leadership and management skills, I am using the same skills and concepts of counseling, just with different labels, but please keep that between us.

As I developed the skillsets of both counseling and coaching, I immediately noticed a great deal of overlap between the two disciplines. Today, many clients reach out to me, desiring to work on both areas. To describe the relationship between the two, I often use a scale of -10 to +10 with individual clients, as well as couples, to get a reading on how they feel about their situation overall. When clients seek counseling, it is because their negative emotions are getting in the way of everyday living, and they would rate themselves on the negative side of the number line. The initial goal is to equip them to get back to zero, so they are emotionally stable. If they are on the positive side of the number line (zero to +10), I frame that as coaching, helping clients become effective in emotional intelligence and maximizing their overall quality of life, both intrapersonal and interpersonal. I am hoping to write another book combining the concepts of personality with the "machine" of emotional intelligence, but this book is more focused on the negative side of the number line, counseling.

The Three Foundational Tenets of Daily Emotional Management

Clients reach out to me because they are on the negative side of the number line and their negative emotions are getting in the way of their everyday living. They need help managing their negative emotions. While there are several negative emotions, I use the main emotions of insecurity, anxiety, fear, worry, anger, and depression. In order to equip them fully, we commonly need to address two additional concepts that are impacting their daily emotional management, namely their identity, value, and worth, and the trauma they experienced. I use the word trauma in a general sense, not diagnostically. Any negative experience where healing is needed, I classify as trauma in light of the fact the emotional impact of those negative experiences carries over to several future situations until healing takes place. In each of these areas, we feel a different degree of loss, and we need to recognize it as loss, which gives us permission to grieve. With grieving, there is nothing to "fix", we just need to give ourselves permission to hurt. With the surface, felt emotions of insecurity, anxiety, fear, worry, anger, and/or depression, there is a *loss of the moment*. When we get hit any negative experience and take it personally, there is a *loss of our* worth. Finally, when we experience the immense pain of trauma, there is a *loss to a part of our soul*. Recognize it as loss, it's okay to hurt. Now, before I start walking through how to emotionally manage negative emotions, I want to establish three foundational tenets.

Tenet One: Emotion is Energy

First, *emotion is energy*. I frame emotion this way because I believe emotion is the energy we use to act, but also, I have found that many people have a difficult time being able to accurately label and assess the murkiness of their *emotions* and how to manage them. When we label emotion as energy, we can more easily assess it, understand it, evaluate it, and correct it. From this perspective, I say there is good emotion/energy and negative (not bad) emotion/energy. The good energy is the excitement energy we burn to improve our micro and macro quality of life, which creates greater positive emotions. Negative, again, not bad; emotion/energy is just simply the energy produced in the process of problem-solving. Think of it this way: I have a problem, I'm creating negative consequences, and I want it fixed and want it to go away. Maybe I have a paper to write, I am out of clean underwear, or I'm in an argument with my loved one. Whatever it is, it produces negative energy, and that energy is there to ensure that the problem gets solved. Issues arise when we have too much of either kind of emotion. Too much good energy is overstimulation or addiction to good emotion, such as avoiding responsibilities or creating too much dopamine with video games, entertainment, or substance abuse. Too much negative emotion can be debilitating anxiety, depression, rage, or stress.

The Second Tenet: The Type and Amount of Emotional Energy

From this flows the second tenant, which is the need to correctly label the brand or type of negative emotion, as well as having the right *amount* of emotional energy. Using a scale of one to ten, how much emotional energy does my present situation need? This is determined by evaluating our behavioral response and the energy required for it. Energy is literal physical energy burned in the verbal, nonverbal, or response of action. Having a "10" level of emotional energy is not automatically bad because the amount of energy needed is objectively based on each specific situation. For example, when we heard the news that we were going to be first-time grandparents, our positive energy skyrocketed. It is a joy that only those who get that news truly understand. We cannot wait to spoil that child and hand them back to their parents. Yep, and that's the way it should be, deal with it. If the amount of positive emotional energy stayed at the level when we first heard the news, we would turn into "helicopter" grandparents, and our children would rightfully avoid us like the plague. Conversely, if at some point our grandchild runs out into the street (because of course his parents weren't watching him, hence our need to be helicopters), I assess the situation and ask myself, "Hmmmm, how much energy do I need to address the situation?" That evaluation happens in a millisecond, and I leap with a "10" level to protect my grandchild. The level of energy needed is based upon either the degree of good news I hear or the degree of danger or negative consequences that could result from the situation.

Our Emotional Storms

While it is most common for us to experience an inflation of negative emotion, there are times when the emotional energy is too low, such as a teenager's level of emotional energy when it comes to completing their homework or chores or when a spouse is too passive in romantically pursuing their spouse. The goal is to have the right amount of emotion and energy. People reach out to me because they are troubled by their current status quo, and most of the time, they would define their status quo as suffering from an overwhelming amount of negative emotional energy. There are several reasons why they carry this weight. They either avoid the very action that would burn off the emotional energy, or, more commonly, the amount of their emotional energy is way too high for the areas of their life they attribute to causing the emotional energy in the first place. Most situations may only need a two or three on the scale of importance, but they have a six, seven, or eight level of energy. Even if they did respond effectively, the situation, by definition, can only objectively absorb a two or three amount of energy, so they still "carry" the rest of the energy. More frequently, they unleash all six to eight points of energy on the poor situation (normally a person) and cause damage in some way. We all know what it feels like to both dump that extra energy as well as have that negative energy dumped on us. It's not a pleasant experience. After this dumping, we then have a whole new problem situation on our hands, producing an entirely new package of energy that needs to be burned to recover from the damage caused by the first mistake. This is a very cyclical process and often doesn't get resolved. We get burned out dealing with it and just resign ourselves that it won't get solved, but the negative energy sits inside of us, rotting, until we find a way to solve it or heal from the overall experience.

Causes of the Emotional Storms

While there may be multiple reasons for the exorbitant amount of emotional energy, I believe there are three main causes. Before I delve into the causes, allow me to lay out another key premise. *Emotions don't produce themselves; they come from sentences in our minds.* Those sentences are thoughts and opinions about us, the situation, and the people involved. These statements create the energy based on what is being experienced or what needs to change to create a different experience. These formulas in our mental model fill in all the variables, calculate how to interpret them, and evaluate all the potential outcomes, giving a weight of importance to those outcomes, which produces our emotional energy. The emotional energy is then burned through the expression of joy (if positive emotional energy), or through some action response (if negative emotional energy) to change the status quo of the situation. This process itself is natural. As stated, the problem is not the existence of negative emotion. It is when the emotional energy does not match the objective intensity of the situation. There are three main causes for this inflation of emotion.

First, there is some form of a lie we believe about the situation. If we are looking for a job, for example, we may believe the lie and say to ourselves, "I'll never get a job!" If we are having a difficult time in a relationship, we insert lies about the other person, wrongly judging their motives for example, or believe lies about ourselves such as "I'm an idiot, I ruined the relationship." The various interpretations motivate us to choose certain paths. We choose non-RHWR paths because we believe these lies about the situation. Even if we are practicing impulse control and successfully choose an RHWR path, the inflated negative energy doesn't dissipate, keeping us escalated. Why? Where do you burn emotional energy to solve a lie? The only way to reject it is by replacing it with statements that are true. For example, if I believe I'll never get a job, I will replace it with statements of truth, such as, "The truth is I did not try as hard as I should have in high school and college, so I don't qualify for the jobs I want. However, I could finish college or go to trade school, and if I work hard in any job, I can get promoted. I just may have to accept a job I don't want now to eventually get the job I do want." The goal is not to replace lies with positive statements but with truth. I am all about giving and providing hope and encouragement, but it must be based on truth. I would love to say to myself, "I am the greatest golfer in the world." It certainly is positive, but it isn't true. Jesus said that the truth would set you free (John 8:32), not positive, motivational statements. However, you can make positive emotional statements to yourself that would be effective, such as, "I will be confident. I am tenacious. I will be successful." Then, form your mental model strategy based on truth to get you there!

I have also observed another emotionally damaging trend among clients. Clients could process a story objectively and truthfully, but they end with either a question or a statement that isn't true or provable, and it has the same negative effect of creating a large amount of negative emotion that has no outlet. I have a client who struggles with anxiety about her health and the health of her family. She had a mammogram, and her doctor told her it came back clear. She concluded, "But what if he's wrong?" Her mind concluded the story of her mammogram with a question that produced doubt, to which her mental model then responded logically with a great deal of anxiety and fear. I asked her to answer her own question with truth, *i.e. is he wrong?* Another client processed a situation and then concluded with, "I don't think I had integrity in that situation." In this case, it wasn't a question, but a conclusion where she judged herself. I advised her to "prove" to me that she didn't have integrity. Whenever we make character evaluations about ourselves or others that aren't action-based but an overall evaluation based on a series of behaviors, we conjure up stories in our minds that we use to back up the claim. However, we need to prove that all those statements or examples are either true or RHWR. Even if this client was correct, she still needs to be as specific as possible about where her integrity fell short so she can burn her emotional energy on a specific strategy to rectify it or grow from it. The other point is that she may have made a mistake, but it isn't an issue of integrity, or she may be wrong altogether, and the truth is she couldn't have responded any better. Truth is the goal, because it produces the right words to describe it and produces the right amount of emotional energy because it is the product of an action strategy to respond to the true statements, opinions, and conclusions about the topic at hand.

Mental Model Formula Formation: *Build self-awareness what sentences of interpretation your mental model is producing and replace all lies with truth.*

The second major cause of the emotional storms is related to our identity, value, and worth (IVW). I will take an entire chapter to walk through the formation of our IVW and how to take control over it. But for the sake of my point, I will simply say that our emotion gets inflated because when we have a negative experience, like a mistake or failure or someone pointing out a flaw, we make the mistake of taking it personally. We have all taken things personally and have observed people in the process of taking things personally. What does it even mean to "take it personally"? I frame it with the concept of IVW. The negative event impacted the person's perceived value and worth. It wasn't simply a weakness or mistake that needed to be corrected; it became a reflection of their reputation and identity as a person. Somehow, they decided that their value and worth decreased from that negative experience.

Our mental model produces to achieve both the micro and macro emotional goals as well as the assessment of our own value and worth. Our present tense feeling is made up of both mood and emotion, evaluating the present probabilities of achieving our micro and macro emotional goals. *Our mood is an overall summation of our most recent successes and failures in moving closer to our ideal quality of life.*

When it comes to the overall evaluation of our value and worth, who has the authority and influence to add their opinions? There are many of us who are too concerned about what other people think, and there are many of us who don't care enough about what people think. The most mature among us absolutely care what others think of them, but also don't let it impact their value and worth as a person. Because the negative truth doesn't impact their value and worth, they are free to proactively seek out that information with the goal of eradicating the blind area and being better equipped in the growth process. Our ultimate goal is to have our subjective view of ourselves perfectly match the truth of how others see us and, more importantly, how God sees us (objective). More on this later.

The final cause for our emotional storms is because of prior trauma. Like IVW, I will take an entire chapter on the topic of trauma. Trauma can either be official, diagnosable trauma, which must be at a high enough level that threatens our long-term physical or emotional well-being, or it can simply be an emotionally intense experience that has long-term effects. As a professional, I completely understand diagnoses, but I try to help the client focus on the actual behaviors that need to change because of the human tendency to link the diagnosis to their value and worth and make the mistake of defining themselves through the lens of a diagnosis that is only temporary. Although it may be a permanent part of their DNA, e.g. a personality disorder or something biologically based like schizophrenia, it does not define their value or worth, nor is it their destiny. The same is true with the label of "trauma" because I have seen so many people do the same with that identity, which seems to give them the feeling of being stuck with it, which permanently decreases their value and worth. The difference is that while IVW is derived from within, trauma is derived from without, i.e. our environment or caused by other people. Our emotions get inflated because we experience a situation, and our mental model realizes this current situation is very similar to what happened before (the trauma). When that happens, our mental model acts like a backhoe, scoops a huge pile of emotion from the trauma, and dumps it right on this current situation.

The Third Tenet: All Negative Emotion is Exposing Something in Me

Now we get to the big one. All that negative emotion is exposing something in me. At first blush, that sounds bad, but it is not. That's because it takes the power and authority over our emotions from the environment and gives it back to us. And much more powerfully, it is the doorway to the journey of our greatest growth. Let's imagine my wife does something that upsets me, which everyone who knows us knows my wife never has and never will do something to upset me. Whenever we argue, we aren't arguing but simply discussing one of Greg's shortcomings (just playing it safe, folks). But let's say, for instance, she does something that upsets me. What do I do? What do we all do? My first response is to start processing what my wife did or did not do that did not fulfill my expectations. "How dare her!" But I don't stop there, oh no. I start reflecting how her mistake is related to some character flaw. I then start to really churn through the emotional energy by judging her motives. By now I am really consumed, attacking her in my mind and my heart, thinking of ways to get justice. More than that, I am forcing the solution to my emotions to squarely rest in her changing. Well now I am stuck because I have just concluded the solution to my negative emotion rests in something outside of my control.

That isn't to say that there is not something legitimate that I need to address with her. I am saying that the first step in this process is to first discover what is being exposed to me. I must sift through all those interpretations and opinions my mental model produces, figure out which ones are true versus not, and ensure that all response paths pass the RHWR grid. Once that is completed, I can then come to her with my rational point of frustration. If I just go to her with my first reactive, impulse response of emotions, it is going to be a lot of emotional energy, and that is when I cause damage to her and our relationship and frankly, she doesn't deserve me to treat her like that. But don't worry, she's not helpless. After I do that, she is going to boomerang that emotional energy right back and educate me on how I psychologically blew it. All of that emotional energy that I so easily whipped up came from 1) my legitimate point of frustration, 2) several lies I may be believing about myself and her, 3) a need to defend myself because I may have allowed her offense to decrease my value and worth, or 4) that situation triggered a mental model memory from long ago where I felt vulnerable and exposed from some outside force more powerful than me.

Even if I successfully walk through this process, I need to figure out why my mental model produced that initial response in the first place. What "buttons" did she push? What insecurities did she expose in me? You can immediately see why we must first figure out what is being exposed in us before we can legitimately respond to any situation, and I'm sure you can feel how hard this process can be because all of these causes are nestled deep within us and have created a network of formulas that need to be recalculated and re-wired. Finally, it may seem daunting to you because you have already suffered many consequences from these emotional storms. Take heart, that is exactly why I am writing this book. The Lord God above lends us His brilliance to help ourselves and others be much more effective in our emotional management. The result is more confidence in our identity, value, and worth, and we become stronger than we ever have being healed from the intense trauma we experienced. Now that the three tenets have been set, we move to the process of daily emotional management and unpack the emotions of insecurity, anxiety, fear, worry, anger and depression.

Chapter 4
The Matrix Of Insecurity

The emotion that most closely aligns with the truth that all negative emotions are exposing something in us is insecurity. When insecurity applies to our emotions, I will use the definition: *something that is not firm or fixed, unsteady*. This, I believe, is the gateway to the rest of the negative emotions as it relates to the foundation of our security, value, and worth. Insecurity may be the base, or foundational level of the emotions in this book, but it is the richest as far as revelatory information. Insecurity means we are not firmly founded in the facts about ourselves, whatever those facts may be. It is also related to the emotional intelligence skill of self-regard. Self-regard is the ability to respect and accept yourself—essentially liking the way you are.[3] We have an objective view of ourselves, our strengths and weaknesses, and we continue to work on ourselves. We accept where we are and are not trying to hide our weaknesses or inflate our strengths. Insecurity would then be something we don't like about ourselves, but that is not the only component, since every person on earth, ever,

---

[3] Stein, Steven J.; Book, Howard E.. The EQ Edge: Emotional Intelligence and Your Success (p. 68). Wiley. Kindle Edition.

doesn't like some things about themselves. Well, except for those with certain personality disorders, which we won't get into here. The issue is not that we don't like something about ourselves; it is that we don't want anyone to point out or expose that thing. Like the blockbuster movies, the *Matrix* of insecurity describes the contrast between the experienced world and the real world. The experienced world is where all the focus and energy centers on the people who "made us" feel insecure. The real world is the unattractive world that shows us the real reason those comments have so much power.

Another foundational defining moment for me was when I was 14 years old and was working at the local hamburger joint in Schoolcraft, MI. I was the classic super sarcastic teenage guy, but all of us who worked there were friends and readily "talked trash" with each other. However, one time I took it too far, and I teased this girl so badly I made her cry. That's not the worst of it. As she's walking away, crying, I yelled out to her, "You wouldn't get so pissed off if it wasn't true!" Don't judge me. That moment was an epiphany for me because I turned what I yelled to her on myself. I said, "Oh my gosh, Greg, every single time somebody cuts you down and you get defensive, get angry, and lash out, it's because it's true!" As with the other moments of revelation I mentioned, I started seeing that same truth apply to everyone. When people are either just teasing each other, or when they really are upset, and want to insult one another and cut each other down, they choose to use information about that person that is negative and has truth to it. I have also observed situations when someone tried to insult another person, but the response by others was one of shock, saying "What are you talking about? That person is nothing like that." Or we use another form of sarcasm and tease someone by saying something that obviously isn't true, and everybody just laughs and agrees (because everyone knows it's not true). What I want to uncover is what's behind the true negative emotion of insecurity and how to respond to it.

There are three categories to insecurity. 1) It's true, but I don't want it exposed, 2) it's not true, but I believe it to be true, or 3) true or not true, someone is gossiping about me, and I'm insecure about what others are thinking and saying about me. If there is something I don't like about myself, whether it be a weakness, a failure, a physical feature, or my lack of success in any area, and someone points it out, what do I do at that moment? Well, if it's true, there's nothing to do but own it. Why hide it? Why get upset when someone points it out? It's true, so just agree with it and say you agree that you wish it was different. Throughout the years, I developed a strong dislike of the times someone had power over me and my emotions. It took a long time, but I kept asking myself, "Why am I giving them this much power?" Instead of evaluating and processing them, and attacking them in my mind, I started to figure out what was truly being exposed about me. The issue was in my emotional responses, not in other's choices. I don't want to give anyone, or anything in the environment, the ability to do something, and then have me spend an incredible amount of time and energy responding to it, intrapersonally or interpersonally. Worse than this is when it's not true, but I believe it to be true. These normally come in broad-stroke insults like, "You're ugly, you're stupid, you're an idiot," etc. These insults are normally the insults that bullies use to gain power over another person. I have found the most effective response to these types of insults is to simply say, "Umm, okay." The only way for these insults to work would be for us to get angry and defensive, but we all know if we do that, it never achieves the desired emotional goals of peace and confidence because our negative response solidifies the lie in our mental models.

The last example deals with how to respond to gossip. Sadly, I developed this skill while I was a pastor. People gossip everywhere there is a community of people, including in churches. There are always those people in our lives who don't like us and actively try to hurt us. One common way is to openly discuss those negative items about us, whether they be true or not. I recommend avoiding trying to control the gossiper. Of course, we should make every effort to build a relationship with those who think poorly of us, but sometimes that is not an achievable goal. Once I did everything I could to repair and develop that relationship, but to no avail (they kept gossiping), I then started to process what I was insecure about, namely the impact their gossip would have, so I turned my attention to those listening to the gossip. There are basically three groups of people that would hear this information: 1) those who love me, 2) those who don't know, or barely know me, or 3) those who somewhat know me, but they only have a limited exposure to me. I didn't even worry about those who loved me or those who didn't know me because those who loved me would either push back against the gossiper, ignore it, or come and tell me about it. Those who don't know me will just act confused and long for the conversation with the gossiper to be over. The only group I concerned myself with were those who somewhat knew me. It was always a case-by-case example, but if I cared about what those people thought about me, I would proactively engage those people and simply own the truth. If it wasn't true, I'd simply ask them to have an open mind that what they heard may not be true about me. There are many other techniques to apply here, but the overall point is to not be afraid of what is true, own it, and if you can change it, work on it, and go from there. Take the power away from the environment by having little to no negative emotion because you don't have any insecurities. Is it possible not have any insecurities? I absolutely believe the answer is yes. It is a great place to be. I have not perfected this in every situation, but I'm close, and even when I do blow it, it is easy to recover.

There was no better place to train others in these skills than my work at the Residential Treatment Center. As I stated, I mainly worked with teenage girls, and insecurities were alive and well with these wonderful young ladies. One girl would cry out to me, "Dr. Greg, tell her to shut up because she's really pushing my buttons!" I would reply, "Well, uninstall your buttons. The issue isn't that she's pushing your buttons, the problem is you have buttons she can push." Another time, a girl complained to me that another girl called her a b****. I replied in a similar way when I told her that the issue is not that she called you that, it's that you agree with her, and you didn't want her to point it out. I also highlighted the fact that if it wasn't true, all of the girls who were near her would have defended her, saying something to the effect, "What are you talking about? She is one of the sweetest girls on this unit!" However, strangely, the other girls didn't feel compelled to do that. In another scenario, several of the girls were escalating because one particular girl was "talking trash" and bullying a number of the girls. I called the girls together and said, "Girls, I'm going to give you permission to do or say whatever you can to trigger me. I'll even give you permission to swear at me, just don't attack me physically, but go for it, give it your best shot." They immediately responded with a look of shock, but jumped on the opportunity and said, "Okay Dr. Greg you f'ing have a big nose and your hair's thinning. You have a dad bod and you're so ADHD extra!" On a side note, many girls called me "extra," but I always told them I had no idea what that meant, but it sounded like a compliment, so I thanked them. In response to these girls, I simply said, "Girls, everything you said is true, absolutely true, I own it. Now what?" Literally every girl, even the "mean" ones, just shrugged their shoulders and said, "I don't know, nothing."

It may seem to you that these responses lacked empathy, but I already developed trust and rapport with these girls first before I had freedom to be this honest with them. Further, I would have regular conversations with them teach these same principles in our group therapy sessions. *The goal was to empower them and believe that their environment, whether it be their unhealthy home, school, or even the RTC, has no power over them if they choose not to have power over them.* If their environment does expose a truth, then they need to have the right amount of negative emotions and own it, apologize for it, promise to work on it, etc. Negative emotions are healthy and valid if they are the right type and the right amount. If the criticisms are not true, then nothing is being exposed, and if we all realize that if the criticism is not rational, healthy, wise, or right, *then it is exposing the criticizer, not the one being criticized.* I get frustrated with our current culture, because it places the entire responsibility of the management of our negative emotions on everyone but us. I/we are responsible for our actions, especially if they are not RHWR, but just because I am responsible for my actions, that does not make me culpable for your emotions, nor do your non-RHWR actions make you responsible for my emotions. I gladly and willingly free you from all burden, concern, or responsibility for my negative emotions!

A great example of this is displayed in the unpleasant topic of bullying. All the propaganda and teaching centers around stopping bullying behaviors. I am not here to take away from that, but I am absolutely proposing that we should have just as much, if not more, promotion that screams, **"Stop being bullied."** If you are being "hated" or bullied, burn your emotional energy by trying to figure out why those people have any emotional impact on you, to begin with. Psychologically, how does it work? Someone insults you, whether it be true or not, and you get triggered. Why? It can only be because of one of the reasons I stated earlier. The most common bullying technique these teenage girls would use on one another would be the childish, "You're ugly and fat." When it came to being "ugly," I would ask them if they realized that in the not-too-distant future, they would either date or marry a guy who would be all over them 24/7, and they would wish they were uglier. I say that a bit tongue-in-cheek, but it's a completely subjective evaluation. I still wanted to enforce that the key underlying issue, not only for them, but for all of us:

Mental Model Formula Formation: *The issue isn't what they think of you, the issue is what you think of you.*

Does this negate any negative emotions or hurt from these comments? Of course not, it minimizes them. When it comes to the insult of being "fat" I would ask them to think of a scenario where they went to their doctor for an annual checkup. I asked them plainly, "Would the doctor address your weight with you?" If so, then feeling bad about the weight is a matter of insecurity where you don't want it exposed. What if, when a bully would call you that, you replied with, "I agree. I went to the doctor, and he talked to me about it. I've connected with a nutritionist and just signed up for a gym membership to deal work on it." What would the bully say while stunned at your response? "Oh, well good job." Is that bully wrong? Of course, these precious girls don't have any control over the bully, but they do have control over their response to the bully. The success of this entire premise lies in being able to take the power away from the environment; as well as having the security and confidence to walk into what is true. The truth will set you free, and lies will keep you in bondage. People can be crushingly hurtful, but so can we. Whenever I noticed myself being extremely bothered and upset by someone, I trained myself to switch from burning energy processing them to figuring out why I was so emotional about it. I would keep asking myself the question, "What is being exposed in you, Greg?" and would not let myself off the hook until I found that answer. The answer always resulted in the fact that I felt one of my emotional goals was being blocked. I wanted to be respected, loved, pursued, sought out, validated, encouraged, etc. Whatever it was, my negative opinion of what someone did or didn't do was RHWR, but the amount of negative emotional energy I had was *way* too inflated. It was my issue, not theirs. I wanted to take the power away from my environment, and the only way I could do that was to walk into my negative emotions and come face-to-face with my own insecurities. My insecurities were not their issue to solve. It was my responsibility to solve them. Our culture can continue to try and force everyone to mold themselves to other's insecurities, but it will never work in the end. Why? For one, everyone inherently knows they are not responsible for other's insecurities, especially if they are being asked to respond to that insecure person in ways that are irrational, unhealthy, unwise, and/or just plain wrong. Additionally, the insecure person will never find peace by placing all of the power into the environment.

Mental Model Formula Formation: *Nothing bothers me, unless it should.*

I encourage clients to repeat this phrase to themselves over and over. It is much more difficult to try and walk backwards from a level of high emotional intensity, figuring out what is being exposed and then landing on the right amount of negative emotional energy. I'm teaching you is to train your mental model to *impulsively* go through the door of figuring out what is being exposed in you instead of the natural impulse of standing outside, looking at everything and everyone in the environment, and passing blame and accusations out like a deck of cards. *Start* with "nothing bothers me" and then assess the entire situation through RHWR, and then land on the right amount of emotional energy. Remember the mental model process. Our formulas gather the information in each situation, interpret it, and then create a certain amount of emotional energy to proactively or reactively respond to the situation. If our automatic assumption is that something needs adjusted in us first before something needs to be adjusted in us first before something needs to be fixed in our environment, we are going to live much more confident and peaceful lives.

Two Techniques to Reclaim the Power

The "Have Faith" Technique

Do you have anyone in your life that drives you crazy? They just keep making comments and arguing with you. I want you to have faith, but I don't mean have faith in God. How many times have you begun a sentence in your mind with, "I can't believe they . . ."? How many times have you begun a sentence that way when you think about them? Well, start believing; have faith. The fact that you are still shocked they say what they say or do what they do is kind of more of your issue, not theirs, right? The technique starts with changing the time direction of your emotional energy. Instead of processing what they *did*, think ahead and predict what they are going to do, or are going to say. If you have a spouse or sibling who shares your grief, team up with them and make dollar bets with one another. Think ahead to the next interaction you will have with that person and start brainstorming what you think they will say or do if any given topic comes up. If the topic of your children comes up, what will they say? You will say, "I think they will say . . ." and your spouse/sibling will say, "No, I think they will say . . .". Well bet on it. When the time comes, and that person puts their lack of emotional intelligence on full display, what do you think your auto-response will be at that moment. First, before the statement or response is completed, you will have gleeful anticipation, excited to see who's right. When the response is revealed, you with either say, "Yes! I was right!" or "Shoot! I thought I had that one!" That person will be confused so all you have to say is, "Sorry, inside joke!" Prepare by considering what the most RHWR response would be if they respond with option A and the most RHWR response if they respond with option B. I do not mean the response that will be the greatest comeback or "burn", because that would not pass the RHWR grid. Our goal here is not to win an insult contest, but respond in the most effective way, the most emotionally intelligent way, the most RHWR way. It is the response that is the most mature, the most RHWR response. Think back to Chapter One and achieve the two goals of grace and truth. Make sure your response is like a grace-truth-grace response. You can say something like, "I understand your frustration, but the truth is . . . but I can see your point too." Think about the difference in the emotional experience before and after using this technique. You have completely taken the power that person had over you to trigger you emotionally, and now are completely equipped to have that person have a minimal negative emotional impact on you. Whatever those people have said, it was probably exposing some insecurity in you, whether what they said contained some element of truth, or contained no truth. Either way, it drove you crazy, right? Why? You don't have any control over them, you only have control over your intrapersonal and interpersonal responses.

Embrace the "Digs"

What do you do when people make comments that are simply a one-liner insult or "dig"? I have had people in my life that were like this. I remember going absolutely insane each time they would throw that grenade in my direction. Using the "exposed" principle, I kept asking myself what was being exposed in me and would hold myself accountable and say to myself, "Greg, the fact that you get so upset when they do that is not their issue, it's yours. Why are you giving them so much power over you?". When people use these one-liners against us, it is so easy to start attacking their character and motives. Many of those judgments may have some merit, but is attacking them in our minds the most RHWR path to achieve the emotional goal of confidence and security? Of course not, but that is such a common path we use, with very little fruit at the end of that path. The most effective technique I created was to respond to their digs by embracing them and exaggerating them. I didn't even bother trying to differentiate with them whether what they said was true or not true, I simply would agree with them and exaggerate it. For example, if someone said to me when I was in ministry, "Well, a more seasoned pastor wouldn't do that" I would simply say, "Oh my goodness, you are right. I have some serious immaturity issues! I'm surprised the Board of Elders haven't called me in to address it with me!" When you agree with it and exaggerate it, they are left speechless because you have completely sucked all the negative energy out of the comment. After, they don't have any more emotional fuel to keep it going. When I began practicing that technique, the results were amazing. It made the situation super light, and many times, we both laughed. Try it! Now if what they said had merit, I would absolutely walk away owning it and would work on it. If it wasn't true, then it ended right there. I simply quit walking the pathway of defending myself, trying to convince someone else to think differently of me. However, it always depends on the person. Sometimes I would respond with this technique, and if their comment was out of character for them, I would follow up and ask them if there was something we needed to talk about. I used the Proactive Teachability technique to remove their defensive mechanisms because maybe they were seeing something I wasn't. This technique is more effective for those people who have an addiction to these grenades. Changing them or having them stop launching the grenades is simply an unachievable goal, and I quit trying to achieve it. Insecurity is at the bottom level of my emotional management system. Our insecurities are always present and may be exposed at any minute. Before moving on to anxiety, I am going to open the basement door and address what's in the basement: the machine of our Identity, Value, and Worth.

Chapter 5
Identity, Value And Worth (IVW)

As I explained earlier, one of the main reasons our negative emotions inflate is because we take things personally. Whenever life does not go our way, or someone makes a comment that shines a light on a weakness of ours, our emotional energy skyrockets. We give those things permission to decrease our value and worth. In this chapter, I will equip you to regain full control and authority over your identity, value, and worth.

When I ask people "what is your identity?" they usually pause for a second to think about it, but eventually they just start describing facts about themselves. That makes the most sense because how else would we describe ourselves? These facts and descriptors of ourselves are not void of emotional importance, because with each of those facts, we consciously or subconsciously assign a value or worth. This is a very natural, good, and healthy process. As a matter of fact, I think it is what every human being on Earth who has ever existed has naturally thought about and spent time processing. Like everything thing else, my psycho-babble mind kicks in, and I ask the question, "Where did the formula for value and worth originate?" I mean, how do we know how much value or worth to assign to facts? This is a completely subjective process, but we still need some objective comparisons to give us a true North. So where did we get the formula in the first place? The raw formula came from our parents. Let me explain. Every relationship must have two things: safety and pursuit. Every relationship, human-to-human, human-to-animal, animal-to-human is based in each creature feeling safe and being pursued by the other person. If a child feels both safe and pursued by his or her parents, the child has a high value and worth. Value and worth would be among the list of good and healthy emotional goals we all are trying to achieve, along with feeling safe and feeling pursued. Pursuit is not only feeling wanted and loved, but it is also what we want to feel when recovering from failure. When we make a mistake, respond poorly, or do something wrong, our parents should come alongside us, correct us, equip us and tell us it's okay. Additionally, our value and worth increase when our parents coach and train us in how to be independent, successful, and mature. Such as teaching us to not cry after we spill our milk, to how to be successful interpersonal relationships, to giving us wisdom in the higher things of life and eternity, learning how to love and be true disciples of the Lord. Children are basically saying to mom and dad, "Look, I have no clue how to do this life thing and I need your help." Right? So, they are trained indirectly by observing our responses to situations, how to grow and mature, how to do relationships, how to be successful, and how to ensure the Lord remains our First Love (Revelation 2:4). We also train them directly in many ways, and hopefully those RHWR principles and truths stick, despite our own lack of adherence to them.

It is beautiful if a child feels pursued by his or her parents, but we all know there is a spectrum of healthy to unhealthy parents.

Sadly, there are children who grow up in unhealthy environments, and they often have low self-worth. Along with our parents, peers become inputs to the formula at some point. It culminates during the adolescent years, and the same principle is true: if we feel pursued, validated, and liked by our peers our value and worth is high. This goes for the opposite as well. Then as we continue to grow, other significant people are added as inputs like teachers, bosses, coaches, boyfriends or girlfriends and so on, and the formula of value and worth culminates with our spouse. Every human being ever must go through this process, and it is unavoidable. Ideally this natural process results in a strong IVW.

Mental Model Formula Formation: *at some point, every person must make the conscious choice to remove every other human being from that formula.*

It must be a deliberate choice. Why? Because if we don't make an intentional choice to remove every other person from that formula, we make our value and worth contingent upon other people pursuing us, validating us, liking us, etc. If my value and worth is contingent upon this happening, I am going to live a very sad life! However, let me be clear about something: removing every other human being from the formula of value and worth does *not* change the definition of relationship, i.e. safety and pursuit. It does *not* change the standard of healthy, successful relationships, and does *not* change RHWR expectations of the various relationships in our lives. *What it changes is the degree of negative emotional impact when that desired pursuit and validation doesn't occur.* Because the power of every relationship is measured by the degree of safety and pursuit, if our expectations are not met in any given relationship for a long enough period, we simply choose to remove that relationship from our lives. That is also a natural process.

To begin the process of removing every human being from the formula of our value and worth, start saying to yourself, *"I don't need them to pursue or validate me; I want them to, but I don't need them to pursue or validate me."* When you do this, you immediately start changing the formula in your mental model. Again, the definition, standards, and expectations of relationships do not change, the only thing that changes is the degree of impact on us if our desires are not meat. Continue to repeat, "I don't need them to pursue me. I want them to, but I don't need them to." As you repeat this in your mind, begin to use the names of specific people in your life. "I don't need my wife to pursue me or validate me. I want her to, but I don't need her to." Then start going through all the key relationships throughout your life, using the same process, ending with your mom and dad. "I don't need my dad to pursue me or validate me; I want him to, but I don't need him to." As you do this more and more, the "weight" of the loss of the lack of pursuit begins to decrease. Also begin to say, "It is no longer devastating that they were the way they were, it's just disappointing." Notice the location of the words "devastating" as opposed to "disappointing." Devastating is something felt inside of me, while disappointing is focused on something outside of me. It is less intense because the object is externalized. I am not devastated; I am just disappointed (in them not being what they should have been or treating me the way they should have).

While you do this process, you also need to start assessing and evaluating *what you think of yourself*. When there is a lack of desired pursuit, we naturally question our own worth. We try to give justification why they should pursue us by pointing out in our minds what we do for that person, how much they mean to us (and they should know that), and how important they are to us. Eventually, if the lack of pursuit continues for an extensive length of time, we often consciously or unconsciously conclude, "It must be something about me. I must not be worth it." What we have to offer them is not worth their effort to pursue us like we want to be pursued. While we internally talk like it is their fault, we emotionally *conclude* that it is because we are not valuable enough or worth enough. Ultimately, the conclusion to this issue is not what anyone thinks of you, it's what you think of you. When you change the words from need to want, you are assuming 100% authority and control over your IVW. To start this process, the first step is to define your identity and make a list of facts about yourself. These facts can be listed under the categories of roles (husband/wife, parent, career, Christian, etc.), accomplishments (education, promotions, etc.), your life values, attributes (personality [strengths/weaknesses] and physical), habits [daily/weekly living] and whatever facts you deem to be a part of your identity. It's your choice. It's an organic list and takes time to develop. Once you make that list, assign a value and worth to each of those facts. You can use whatever value and worth system you want, but I suggest you simply choose *increase*, *decrease*, or *no impact*. It's subjective. Does this fact about me increase my value and worth, decrease my value and worth, or does not impact on my value and worth? It is not a bad thing when we decide that a fact in our identity decreases our value and worth. Each of those facts can be categorized in one of two columns: control and no control.

    First, if a particular fact about ourselves is in the "no control" column, then we must figure out why a fact about ourselves we have no control over decreases our value and worth. A simple example would be a physical feature about us that decreases our value and worth. It is completely okay not to like a particular feature or wish it was different, but it should not have the degree of impacting our value and worth. The problem is what you think of you. We must address why we have the negative emotions we do in this area, and why these negative emotions are so inflated. Even if there are features about myself that I do not like, I would ask myself the question, "Is there anyone that has physical features more undesirable than me but are completely content and at peace with those physical features?" Of course! So, the issue that needs addressed is the interpretation of those physical features we cannot change, not the physical features themselves. This obviously does not apply to physical features we do have control of, like personal hygiene or health issues brought on by poor choices. The stories many people tell themselves is how bad other people, our culture and our society are "making" them feel about features they have control of, so it's not their lack of discipline or poor choices that need to change, it is the people pointing out that they may want to consider improving in these areas. Our culture promotes, "If you make me feel bad, that means you're bad." Have you ever been frustrated with the cycle of addressing a legitimate frustration you have with someone, and the entire focus of the conversation shifts from the topic of the legitimate frustration to the person being upset with *how* you addressed it? Even if you apologize and own the fact you could have done a better job voicing your frustration, it's nearly impossible to bring the conversation back to the original topic because the person has chosen to sit down in the ashes of the hurt you caused them and wants you to join them at the campfire of pain for a few days to process how this most recent experience is reflective of their life story and how the story needs to be retold adding this current chapter to their book. That process starts to make your eye twitch because all you want to do is address the frustration and ask for a simple change, but it seems the person needs to first heal from a lifetime of negative emotions before he or she can fix this issue. You then get angry, point that out, with more intensity, and now another chapter needs to be added to the book. I asked if you have ever had this experience to get you to think about someone in your life where that is the pattern and get your buy-in. Now may I ask if you're *that other* person? If I asked the same question, with the same scenario, to those closest in your life, would they think of you?

Resiliency and Tough-Mindedness

Formula Formation: *Change your focus from the validity of your pain to the degree of your pain.*

To truly master our negative emotions, we need to switch our focus from the environment, the other person, or anything we simply do not control. Our negative emotions are many times triggered by our environment, but the solution is *not* in our environment. Something deeper may be being exposed in us, that is why we need to shift from focusing outward to focusing inward. We need to shift our focus to first figuring out what is being exposed in us by 1. correctly naming the blocked emotional goal, 2. labeling the correct negative emotion we are feeling (explained later), and 3. arriving at the correct quantity of negative emotion (intensity) this situation requires. The correct quantity of (emotional) energy is defined by the amount of (emotional) energy that needs to be burned physically to have the most effective behavioral and/or verbal response. Read that again. This is the summary of it all.

There is an incredible amount of emotional energy burned inside our minds and hearts in the process described above. The goal of this book is to help you, over time, to need less and less energy to go through this process. The gateway, the door, to this process is to own the fact you are blind to many things and to be motivated (or freaked out) into passion and desperation to seek wisdom, insight, and understanding.

The first "room" is insecurity, and we need to take a trip to the basement before going into the other rooms. We have established the components of identity, but I am taking time to review the process, to leap up to 30,000 feet and see the big picture because so much of this material is a deep dive into the minutiae. As we go through the minutiae, I need to stop and insert crucial points that need to be learned and absorbed into the mental models for processing all this information. We are at one of those points now. We need to change our focus from the *validity* of our emotions to the *degree* of emotion. When we are focused on the validity of our emotions, we try to prove that our negative emotions are legitimate. Why would we need to do that? The only possible reason is that there is an external force challenging us, and we feel compelled to validate why we are upset. First, release yourself from the burden of validating the existence of your negative emotions. You have them, so they exist. Remember *goal* and *path*. Your emotional goal is to alleviate the existence of these negative emotions; choosing the pathway of burning a lot of emotional energy on validating them does not pass the RHWR test. Additionally, where is the focus of this process? On the environment, on the external, on what you don't have control over. Addressing this comes at the end, but when it comes to negative emotions, we are obsessed with this being the first step. Turn around and go back inside by walking through the door above. Finally, and ironically, if we really listened to what the person was saying, they aren't disagreeing with the existence of our negative emotions; they are disagreeing with our impulse non-RHWR response to the negative emotions driven by the inflation of the negative emotions. However, because of our neuroticism and self-absorption, we only interpret them as invalidating our negative emotion. Turn around and go inside by walking through the door above.

Now, we focus on the degree of our negative emotions. This is different than the three common causes of inflated emotion (lies, IVW, and trauma). Before we address these items, I believe we have to do an honest intrapersonal self-assessment on our degree of resiliency and tough-mindedness. The definition of resiliency is an ability to recover from or adjust easily to adversity or change[4]. What correlates with resiliency is tough-mindedness, which is a person who is realistic or unsentimental in temper or outlook[5]. I believe these skills are developed over time. We develop these skills or don't develop these skills, from our parent's training. The first time this training occurs is when we are infants, and we cry not because we need anything but because we want attention. I won't say that it is because we want comfort because that implies there is something negative happening that we need comfort from. We cry because we want to increase our quality of life by being held, using the RHWR

---

[4] "Resiliency." Merriam-Webster.com Dictionary, Merriam-Webster, https://www.merriam-webster.com/dictionary/resiliency. Accessed 20 Jul. 2024.

[5] "Tough-minded." Merriam-Webster.com Dictionary, Merriam-Webster, https://www.merriam-webster.com/dictionary/tough-minded. Accessed 20 Jul. 2024.

path of crying. From that point on, our parents trained us how to respond to each negative situation (whether physical or relational) by teaching us how to interpret each situation. What about the situation is wrong? How big of a deal is it? What are the best responses to the situation? They *should* teach us not only their conclusion on how weighty it is but *why* it carries the weight it does, and then encourage us if our response didn't match what was RHWR. Obviously, the response of "Don't be such a baby!" or "Oh my gosh! My poor baby!" doesn't pass the RHWR test. The opposite could also be true when we respond with *less* negative emotion than we should, such as, "You need to realize how bad you hurt their feelings." Sure, there are some who grow up with low empathy. But I am not going to address this because, well, there's no way those people would read a book like this.

A person's maturity is directly correlated with the size of the thing that upsets them or causes them anxiety. While assessing someone's maturity is somewhat nebulous, it seems we immediately know when there is a lack of it, observed by the degree of their negative emotional response to the troubling situation. When I worked at the RTC, I had to come up with metaphors and analogies on the spot to make my point with the teenagers. One of my favorite analogies to help clients step out of themselves was to have them envision a person yelling insults out to a line of five to ten people. The person on one end is getting very angry, crying, and yelling back at the bully, while the person on the other end is not responding at all other than just slightly shaking his head. Everyone in between is responding with varying levels of intensity, in order, from low to high. I asked my client what the difference was between each of the individuals, if they were all experiencing the exact same stimuli, with the exact same repercussions? While it could be because of the insult, it is also caused by their degree of resiliency and tough-mindedness. I have worked with people across the resiliency and tough-minded spectrum, and those with the lowest levels are in the greatest danger because they grow at such a slow rate. They grow slowly because they are consumed with only processing the environment and how much the environment hurt them. Worse than that, they have no ability to "move on" because their recovery is contingent upon the environment, making its sole obsession the hurt it has caused and doing everything it can to make up for it. It is a very powerless state to be in, but they have seemingly been trained (enabled) their whole lives to place all culpability of their negative emotions onto others. We are all familiar with the contrast between how parents respond to their children's bad grades or getting in trouble at school with newer generations compared to the generations of old. I cannot emphasize enough that the goal is NOT to have a low level of negative emotions. That would not be RHWR. The goal is to have the right amount. What is the right amount? Intrapersonally, inside of me, there is no right amount because this energy is automatically produced from our mental models. Whatever the amount of negative emotional energy, the key is to burn that energy by first figuring out what is being exposed in us. Only after we exhaust this process and arrive at an RHWR conclusion can we assess the right amount of interpersonal energy we need to respond effectively to our environment.

Formula Formation: *Has there ever been anyone who has either had it harder or experienced something worse than what I am, and yet came out stronger or was successful?*

Here is another defining moment for me. After I graduated with my bachelor's degree (I was in the nine-year program), I realized that I was the first person in my family to graduate with a bachelor's degree. On top of that, I was accepted into seminary and would soon begin to work on my master's degree. I was excited but overwhelmed. I was a youth pastor at the time, and in one of my regular meetings with my senior pastor, I was vomiting all of this emotion, and I distinctly remember him sitting in his desk chair, kind of leaning back, slouched, with a slight grin on his face and a confused look in his eyes. He interrupted me and said with a low, soft, and slow sarcastic tone, "Wellllll Greg, you're not walking a road that thousands haven't already walked before." I sat there stunned and embarrassed. First, because I instantly realized how emotionally immature, I was being and second, I was freaking out in front of a guy who had his doctorate, pastored churches for 30 years, was a president of a mission organization and a Bible college and started a seminary at that college. From that moment on, I developed the question that I have used with myself and countless others to help them see themselves objectively, recognizing others have walked similar and even much harder paths. By realizing this, their emotional energy shifted from processing how hard they had it to figuring out what everyone else did to be successful. Again, their focus went from the environment where they had no control to figuring out what was happening inside of them and creating an effective strategy of response.

This may seem like a major tangent, but it's not. I stated that our first action step is removing every other person from the formula of IVW. We need to start saying to ourselves, "I don't *need* them to pursue or validate me. I want them to, but I don't need them to."

The success is not measured by how many times we repeat it, but by how much it benefits us by decreasing the negative emotional impact on us when we aren't pursued or validated by others. I want you to be aware of the factors involved in your ability to experience this, which are the three causes of inflation, and your levels of resiliency and tough-mindedness. Next, I want to equip you with a proactive way to solidify your independence in your IVW, which will fully remove others from having any access to it.

The Triangle

I've created a triangle that contains the three areas that should make up our IVW. The top point is God. Regardless of your religion, if you believe in a creator, which most of humanity does, a major portion of your IVW comes from what you think God thinks of you. I have formed and perfected these concepts through my own journey. In Christianity, we often state to one another that our identity, our sufficiency, and our needs are all met in Christ. This is a powerful truth within Christianity, but to be completely transparent and honest, getting to the point where we actually experience these truths is a difficult process. The only way to arrive here is for the Christian to come face-to-face with the fact that they are not the source to have these needs met, and neither is any other person in their life.

The Miracles that formed IVW

For me, this journey was one of profound importance to my emotional and spiritual development. I have always had this undercurrent where I was disappointed in how little I felt pursued by others. Whether it be my personality or early experiences, I knew that the best relationships I observed were those who went to great lengths to make the other person feel special. Considering this, I pursued people greatly (or at least I felt I did), and over time became disillusioned with the realization that it wasn't reciprocal (or at least I felt it wasn't). This undercurrent, through several other circumstances and experiences, led to me having an emotional affair after I left the ministry. Once it ended, I was left devastated, experiencing deep shame and guilt. What's worse, I was married with three children. I was also a pastor and a marriage counselor. How, oh God, how, did this happen? I immediately started seeing a psychologist to answer this question, and in our first session, as I was telling the story and how it might have happened, I complained that I felt I always pursued others harder than they pursued me. In a moment, my frustration culminated, and I yelled out, "I just want them to make my world!" At that very moment, I immediately had a vision from God that showed dozens of dominoes standing on end, and on the top of these dominoes were the faces of everyone I knew in my life. I couldn't make out each face; I just knew they were all people I knew. At that moment, the Holy Spirit, in His true fashion as wind, came and didn't just blow the dominoes over. He blew them off the table and loudly said, "I make your world!" This vision took place in less than two seconds, and it hit my heart hard. I immediately broke and wept intensely. That moment began a deep healing and growth experience that lasted years. At the same time, I was listening regularly to pastors Bill Johnson and Kris Vallotton with Bethel Church in Redding, CA. They are a powerful ministry and have had many miraculous experiences in their church. I was a pastor at a Bible church, and we were known to be non-charismatic (which meant we didn't believe in the practice of tongues, signs, and wonders, but we did believe in miracles). We felt that charismatic churches focused too much on those things for personal change instead of focusing on growth, development, learning, and mind/heart transformation. However, when I was first exposed to Bethel, I was drawn into their approach. While they strongly believed in the pursuit of signs, wonders, and miracles, they strongly believed that the path to those things was through intimacy with the Lord. I was sold. After that vision, I began to strongly pursue intimacy with the Lord. This process included a combination of developing a true image of who the Lord was, which centers on His goodness. Like many people, I struggled with seeing God as sitting on a throne being disappointed in me, but started to see Him as delighting in me as a great father would delight in his own son. His goodness was best displayed in who Jesus Christ is and how Jesus interacted with His followers in the gospels, which foreshadowed how He interacts with us. Because in Jesus dwells the fulness of the Trinity in bodily form (Colossians 2:9), our experience of prayer and worship relationship with God can be viewed and imagined as if we are interacting and speaking with Jesus Himself. Many believers struggle to connect relationally with God because their main image of Him is a powerful being sitting on a throne very far away. He is all-knowing and hard to please. That is the standard image every time a human being creates a religion. On a side note, one the main reasons I believe Christianity is the one true religion is because no one will ever convince me that a human being "thought up" this story. When humans create stories about God, it is always a god who must be appeased. It is a very conditional relationship. Christianity is the only "religion" that has God understanding our condition and loving us so much that He comes down, sacrifices Himself, and takes the punishment for our failure. There is not a human alive, or who has ever lived, that would create a God like that. The best example of how humans image God is in Greek mythology. The gods are infinitely powerful but with human-like weaknesses. It's both laughable and so blatantly obvious we are projecting ourselves onto these gods. In other words, this is what we would be like if we had the same power of God.

Jesus is so powerful because, yes, he is all powerful, but also because he has shown the level of selflessness that no one can ever match or criticize. His entire focus is creating intimacy with us, and it is easy to imagine interacting with Him. So to develop this intimacy with God, I would only picture coming face-to-face with Jesus Himself. Further, I would always engage Him and interact with Him as my First Love (Revelation 2:9), and my Fiancé (developed from the biblical metaphor that He is the bridegroom, and we, the church are His bride). How would the perfect fiancé greet me every time I would engage Him? For sure, it is easier for women to immediately engage Jesus as their fiancé, and it took me some time to adopt that role with Him, but because that is His title for the church, it wasn't that hard. Since I have practiced this, it has been such a beautiful experience, and I can truly, truly say that all my emotional needs are met in God. I truly don't need my wife, my family, my friends, or anyone else to pursue me or validate me. I certainly want them too, but I certainly don't need them to pursue or validate me. My heart and soul have been more peaceful than it has ever been, and it is such a sweet, tender, and precious place to be.

My second miracle occurred one early morning at 3:00 a.m. There was an extended period where I often awoke at 3:00 a.m. from a dream. I started forming the habit of praying, as well as allowing the Holy Spirit to groan in my heart (Romans 8:26), because while my marriage was falling apart, I had no idea what to pray for. During one of these sessions, I had another vision come to me. The scene was an old, white farmhouse, and immediately I found myself in the living room of that house. The living room was lavish and beautiful, but for reasons I can't explain, it was decorated in an old, Victorian age style, with red being the predominant color scheme. The Trinity was off to the side of the living room, standing in front of the entrance to the hallway. I would walk around, talk to the Trinity for a minute, and return to the center of the living room. No one else was there. The Lord spoke to me and said, "Greg, you have spent all of your energy in ministry in the living room, but I want to take you down the hallway." I interpreted this as being a reference to my personality, which is very extroverted and gregarious. Immediately, I was in a dark, dingy hallway. I was musty and could see what looked like old plaster falling off the wall, which revealed the horizonal wooden slats that held the plaster. There was only one light, a little illuminated sphere in the hallway, which I believe was the Holy Spirit. I glanced over my shoulder and saw Jesus with a closed-lip smile on His face, and He said to me, "Don't be scared, I know what you are going to find." Then, doors appeared, two on the left, two on the right, and one at the end of the hallway. I opened each door to find something of meaning in each of the rooms. I debated whether to include in this book what was in each room, but the Lord reminded me that those things were just between Him and me. I will say that when I opened the door at the end of the hallway, it was a door to the universe; it was beautiful. In front of the door, just suspended in space, was a large spool of thread, which was slowly rotating in the direction away from me, and out of the bottom, the threads of the spool were unwinding towards me. But it wasn't just the unwinding of one string, going back and forth as it was unwinding. It was each individual string unwinding towards me, disappearing under the threshold of the door. The Lord said to me, "Whenever you worship Me, you will enter into a different state of consciousness, and your worship will never end." After that vision, I understood the farmhouse was my heart, and the doors in the hallway represented the core components of my heart that led to my identity up to that point. Those doors and what He revealed quieted and settled my heart.

It didn't end there. About two or three months after my vision, I went to a worship and prayer night at an unfamiliar church. I believe a friend of mine told me about it because he knew I was attending the monthly worship and prayer night at my regular church. When I walked in, there was soft worship music playing and people scattered around, praying, journaling, and talking quietly. One of the evening events included a special prayer time where you could sign up and have people pray for you. When it was time, I walked upstairs and into a room with a married couple, and there were three young, college-aged people in the room. I didn't know the couple or the three people praying. We prayed quietly for about a half hour, and the three young people would tell us what they believed the Lord was telling them about us. Each time one addressed me, they said they were hearing from the Lord and conveyed what they heard. Each time they spoke, it was very specific, and I knew exactly what they were talking about, but because they didn't know me, they had no idea what it meant. In Christianity, we believe the Lord will speak to other believers in our lives to give us words of encouragement and direction. This is a very powerful practice but can be greatly abused as you might imagine. That is why we believe the "word" must be very specific and hold details that only the hearer would know the meaning. That is what "proves" it is from the Lord, not from the mind of the one praying. At the very end of the session, one of the girls spoke up and said, "Greg, I have a vision of an old farmhouse. When you go into the farmhouse, there is a beautiful living room, but the Lord doesn't want you in the living room, He wants you in the hallway. In the hallway, there are several locked doors, and the Lord wants you to keep walking up to the doors, and He will open them for you." As you might imagine, I was blown away. Two or three months after I had this vision in my bed at 3:00 a.m., I was in a prayer meeting with people I never met, and one of them repeated to me the exact details of the vision. I was going through the process of a divorce, carving that infamous scarlet letter on my forehead, and feeling like a complete failure as a former pastor and counselor. But God . . .

Some months later, I had a dream in which I saw Bill Johnson standing in a garden area (not vegetable, but a flower garden with chairs), holding a plant that was half-dead, half-alive. He verbally announced the plant would die but human souls live forever. When he said that, I was instantly taken back to the time I was called into ministry when I was wrapping grapes as a Produce Manager. In my dream, I found myself immediately in front of the garden, lying on my side, intensely weeping. What happened next was strange. In my dream, I somehow had the awareness that I was dreaming. I didn't want to wake up, and it's hard to explain, but I came about halfway out of my dream and said in my dream, "Lord, is this You?" He said, "Yes! I'm healing you!" This vision and dream occurred while I was flying around the country doing leadership seminars and executive coaching. My practice was to put my headphones in and listen to worship music. Some time had passed since that dream, and on one late-night flight, I was listening to a worship artist, Misty Edwards. It was very late, and I was barely conscious. Her song *Garden* started to play. The first several words in the song were, "It's You and me alone God. You and me alone. . . I'm a garden enclosed a locked garden . . . Come into Your garden . . . Here O Lord! Have I prepared a place for You!" Right then, I awoke to the Lord saying to me, "Greg, I want you to make a garden area for me in your heart." After I returned home, and for the next couple of weeks, I prayed about what He meant. What was created was a new hallway that went to the left of the door at the end of the hallway that opened to the universe. At the end of the hallway to the left, I created another room from an opening to the left of the new hallway. This room was made of a light tan stone, rough to the touch. In the walls on the right and left, there were one or two backlit alcoves containing vases and other decorations. The floor was made of various squares, about three feet by three feet. When I stood at the large opening to the room, there was a path of squares, made up of the same material as the walls, that led to a throne. Behind the throne were two tall lit lamps. On either side of the path, there was another square, containing decorative landscaping stones, with a small green bush in the center. There was one of those squares on each side, then a stone square, then another square with the stones and a bush. Once the garden room was built, the Lord told me that He was jealous for me, and no one was welcome in the garden but me and Him. From that point on, every time I would worship and pray, it would be in that garden. Since then, I have spent countless hours in that garden, interacting with my First Love

IDENTITY, VALUE AND WORTH (IVW)

and Fiancé. I would go into more detail about what I experienced in that garden, but as He said, no one else is welcome; it's just between Him and me.

These life-changing miracles gave me the courage to do what I needed to do inside of myself, which became the foundation of this entire book:

*Greg needed to leave the **significance** of his **success** in his conscious mind, to walk into the basement of his heart to see what he would find.*

However, for each of you reading this book, you need to do the same, don't you?

_____ *needs to leave the **orderliness** of their **perfection** in their conscious mind, to walk into the basement of their heart to see what they would find.*

_____ *needs to leave the **selflessness** of their **sacrifice** in their conscious mind, to walk into the basement of their heart to see what they would find.*

_____ *needs to leave the **enigma** of their **creativity** in their conscious mind, to walk into the basement of their heart to see what they would find.*

_____ *needs to leave the **wisdom** of their **shrewdness** in their conscious mind, to walk into the basement of their heart to see what they would find.*

_____ *needs to leave the **obedience** of their **loyalty** in their conscious mind, to walk into the basement of their heart to see what they would find.*

_____ *needs to leave the **stimulation** of their **optimism** in their conscious mind, to walk into the basement of their heart to see what they would find.*

_____ *needs to leave the **strength** of their **determination** in their conscious mind, to walk into the basement of their heart to see what they would find.*

_____ *needs to leave the **peace** of their **harmony** in their conscious mind, to walk into the basement of their heart to see what they would find.*

Each of us, in our conscious minds, is pursuing both our micro and macro goals through our personalities and temperaments. I found a lot of safety and security in significance and success, but I had to go into the basement of my IVW and trauma experiences to address some things I was afraid to address. This is my main premise. The negative emotions of insecurity, anxiety, fear, worry, anger, and depression are gateways to these deeper issues. I had to go there in order to find true rest and peace in my heart, but it was worth it.

Back to the Triangle

You can see why our relationship with God is at the top of that triangle. If you don't believe in God, then the other points of this triangle certainly apply, but I also want to speak the truth that you need the Lord. He is good and beautiful. Will you at least pray and ask Him, "If you are there, will please show yourself to me?" That should do it, now just wait.

The bottom left point of the triangle contains your personal and professional goals. Logically and appropriately, a part of my personal value and worth is related to how successful I am at achieving my personal and professional goals. My personal and professional goals are created directly from the list of facts in my identity and those specific facts that have been assigned the value and worth of "decreases my value and worth". With each of those items, create a strategy of the pathway you will execute to change the fact from what it currently is to what you want it to be. Again, you either change the fact itself, or you change your interpretation of that fact if you have no ability to change it (like a physical feature). The issue isn't the physical feature about you, the issue is that you are allowing it to decrease your value and worth.

As you interact more and more with those items and either change your interpretation or create a strategy to improve the item, you first will be surprised by how few items truly decrease your value and worth. Secondly, you will see that the more you define and solidify this process, the less impact your environment will have on you when you don't receive the pursuit and validation you want, or when the environment exposes a weakness or failure. If someone tells you that you have an undesirable feature or a weakness, your auto-response will be to agree with them (owning it) and walk them through your strategy of improvement. You will transition from insecurity to security and confidence.

Finally, the bottom right side of the triangle I call *Pursuit of Self*. The Lord tells us to love our neighbors as we love ourselves (Mark 12:31). This is the second of the two great commandments, the first one being to love the Lord your God with all your heart, soul, body, mind, and strength. Many people don't love their neighbor like they love themselves. However, some who don't love others actually hate themselves. One day, while thinking through this triangle, I thought to myself, "When I am at my absolute best, in each of my roles (husband, father, counselor, professor, Christian, etc.), do I genuinely like that person?" I do like that person. When I am at my best, I like that Greg. So, what do we do about our mistakes, weaknesses, and failures? You may have heard the statement that people define themselves by their failures, and certainly our current weaknesses may be so magnified that they consume a great deal of our time and energy. We may need to go to incredible lengths to bring them under control. However, each of us can't stand it when we fail, proving that it is not who we are at our *core*. Who we are, at our core, is who we are at our best. But considering our weaknesses and bad habits, some aspects of our identity may decrease our value or worth. We need a powerful strategy to move each of those items to *increase*. But again, our failures and weaknesses are not how we are defined and not who we are at our core. We need an objective view of ourselves, using others to help, but only the Lord should define the core of our identity. How does the Lord see us? If we have not yet believed in Him as our Lord and Savior, He sees us as lost sheep and is desperate to have us come back to Him. If we are believers, how does He see us? What does He call us in the New Testament? He calls us saints. (I apologize to my Catholic brothers and sisters; I am already a saint. I don't need to "work" to prove my value and win the title, the Lord already gave it to me). He also calls us priests, kings, friends, children, first love, and fiancé (bride). What He tried to tell us is that we don't have to "work" to become something. That is how the rest of the world thinks. He is trying to tell us *to live out what we already are.* He is trying to get us to understand what our identity already is, and that is why He tells us to *abide* in Him (John 15), and work *out* our salvation, not work to get *to* a more acceptable state.

To put the icing on the cake, look at Romans chapter seven. As you read it, it seems like a glimpse into the Apostle Paul's personal diary. He is struggling, lamenting, and processing how he so desires to do one thing but repeatedly does another. It is truly a powerful description that every believer experiences trying to live out this new identity but continually reverts into the choices of their old identity.

The key explanation he gives (that the Lord told him to give) is that it is no longer he who makes that foolish choice; it is the sin living in him (Romans 7:17). To explain to those who may not know, as Christians, we are new and alive in our spirits, but the physical part of us, our bodies, are not yet renewed, so our "flesh" is still pursuing and desiring sin (or the immediate emotional rewards attached to non-RHWR paths). The process of the Christian training to live out our new identity is to build our emotional and spiritual strength to choose paths that are RHWR by controlling the flesh. Many of you who are not Christians (and many of you who are) have experienced the consequences of Christians failing at this process and hurting you in the process. This is why you may believe the church is full of hypocrites. While I agree that every Christian makes decisions that are hypocritical, there are extremely few who live their lives in such a way as to deserve the title. Further, while God Himself agrees that those who chronically live this way hurt the Lord's reputation, you won't be able to lay that card down when you stand before Him one day to justify your choice to reject Christianity. Sorry. Most Christians can't stand this battle and are desperate to never sin again. If we hurt you or others in the process, we should be quick to apologize. The Lord Himself agrees with this, and that's why He says it's not me (at my core) who is doing it, but the wretched sin living in me. Please don't be foolishly accusatory by saying we are passing off our culpability because that would show that you still aren't getting it. His point is not a removal of accountability; it is a removal of false identity. Even though we are free not to blame our core identity for the failure, the Lord still tells us to count ourselves dead to sin and remove all sin from ourselves, nonetheless. To apply this concept, I say to myself, "*That* Greg needs to die." I want to put to death every part of me that is more committed to the reward of sinful, non-RHWR paths than I am to godly, RHWR paths. The emotional impact of this truth is the same as when someone doesn't pursue me or validate me: it is not devastating; it is just disappointing. I am not devastated because I am not defined by my failures. I no longer annihilate my heart and mind ("I am so stupid!") in my thoughts. I am, however, disappointed in myself and hold myself accountable to the process described in this book to uncover my deep emotional goals, the non-RHWR paths I keep taking to achieve these goals, and slowly, but surely transitioning my affection from the rewards of the non-RHWR paths to the deeper rewards of the paths that are truly RHWR.

Our insecurities are on the surface, exposed through the emotion of defensiveness. Once we address them as described in the last chapter, we need to take a trip down to the basement of our IVW to make this a much more solid, effective, and truthful evaluation machine. Make a list of facts about yourself that you believe make up your identity, assigning a value of increase, decrease, or no impact, and then create a strategy to change (or re-interpret) the facts that decrease your value and worth. Then address where God fits in your identity and what to do about it (I pray you try Christianity), and then start seeing yourself at your best, making that person the predominant person you and others experience.

Chapter 6
That Which Threatens Me

Anxiety vs. Stress

When potential clients contact me, the number one complaint, by far, is they are struggling with anxiety. This is the first example from the second tenant of emotional management, where we must make sure we have the right brand or type of emotion. The label we ascribe to the emotion has a huge impact on how we strategize which path we take to alleviate the negative emotion, thus fulfilling our emotional goal. Many say that anxiety is the cause of their greatly decreased quality of life. When I explain the concept of needing to label the emotion correctly, I lightly tease by saying I kind of feel sorry for anxiety sometimes because it constantly gets thrown under the bus and blamed for everything! Are we really talking about anxiety? Is that really the *main* emotion we are experiencing? To illustrate my point, I met with a client for our first session who said he was struggling with anxiety. He told me it was because he was moving from Virginia to Austin, TX. Prior to meeting with clients for the first time, I ask them to watch a video I created that describes my theoretical approach (the content of this book). Along with the video, I created a PowerPoint presentation they can download and review to better learn the process. I wrote my own definition for each of the emotions, and I define anxiety as the emotion we experience when we are trying to control what we can't control. In my definitions, I don't just describe the traits of the emotions we are experiencing but also the action of response we use (the path) to address the emotion. Anxiety is often produced by a topic over which we don't have control. So, instead of just being okay with the fact we can't do anything about it, we "fret" and think of ways to control it. After my client explained the cause of his anxiety, I asked him, "What are you trying to control that you can't control?" As he explained it, it really had everything to do with everything he had to do to move. I suggested to him that it wasn't anxiety, it was stress. I encouraged him to be as detailed as possible in mapping out a daily schedule detailing what he needs to do every day leading up to the move, and then write a detailed schedule of what time he will leave, when he will eat, what he will eat, when he will stop, where he will stay, etc. If he still has energy, go over every detail of his plan again and add more details. If there are no more details to add, then tell his mental model that every detail is set (that he has control over) and the leftover energy is there to simply execute the plan and start driving. We must understand that our mental model is doing its job. It's simply a machine that reminds us that something is unsettled, undone, or not where we want it to be. This means emotional energy is produced in every area of our lives where there is a paradox. The paradox is simply the gap created when there is a difference between what we believe should be and what is in any particular area.

    I define the emotional energies of anxiety and stress differently. While the feelings of each are strikingly similar, they are very separate because they are based in two very different locations. While anxiety is produced from what we don't have control over, stress is produced from what we do have control over. In other words, stress is in the "control" column, anxiety is in the "no control" column. To determine what emotional label is more accurate, we need to determine if the topic producing the emotion, to begin with, is in the control column or the no-control column. The reason this is so crucial is because our mental models produce a very different suggestion to our frontal lobes between anxiety and stress. If we declare we have anxiety, our mental model responds, "Okay, everyone, it's anxiety! Fire up the fight, flight, or freeze machines!" Even with these responses, we still attempt to control what we can't control by trying to influence that topic or those people who are in the no control column. If we say we are stressed, our mental models try to figure out how to accomplish everything on our task list. If we stall and don't start immediately burning energy completing the task or strategizing how we are going to accomplish the list of tasks, it starts to become overwhelming and absolutely takes on the emotional experience of anxiety. Even if we correctly label everything as being in the control column, the list could be so large that we don't have all the resources (time, money, energy) to do it all, which means we don't ultimately have control over it. The only option in this case is to decrease the number of items through various means, such as delegating them or postponing them, for example. Stress in and of itself is not bad. This would be the one negative emotion that, if you notice, is not on the list of negative emotions because not only is it not bad, but ironically, it is good. With stress, the only evaluation is the amount of stress. We all know stress can be too high. Either the number of items in the control column is too much for us to complete, or we believe the lie that incompletion of the tasks would result in a catastrophe, which means we have failed and our value and worth are impacted. We know we have the right amount of stress when we burn that energy by accomplishing the tasks and arrive at a sense of accomplishment. The segment of the control column that wouldn't necessarily end in a state of complete rest is when the tasks in the control column are a part of a larger topic that has a portion of it in our control and a portion of it out of our control. This happens in relationships (showing love, but not having control over receiving love; or in conflict resolution and problem-solving), in looking for a job (we only have control over influencing others to interview us and hire us but can't control getting the interview or getting the job), or in voting. We can only burn energy influencing but don't have ultimate control over the outcome.

Anxiety is obviously a completely different animal. It is squarely created from the no control column, which is infinitely larger than the control column because what we don't have control over compared to what we do have control over is a ratio too enormous to even spend the energy comparing. When addressing this topic, I am going to go from macro to micro, with the most macro being the things that only God has control over, but under that are things that He allowed to have free will (human beings) and then created a law (the law of freewill) that He committed to not transgressing, which means people have freewill and have the power to choose to do both good or evil, and God will not override their freewill, or else it wouldn't be freewill. Our level of anxiety is a direct result of two things related to this entire column: threat and trust. What topics in your life are producing anxiety in you? The reason you have anxiety is because of a perceived threat from that topic, and you don't have trust in the very agents (other people and/or God) that do have control over these topics. The probability that these agents will act in such a way that is not in your best interest is high (low trust) and the consequences of those actions will harm you in some way (threat).

As described in the last chapter, most of humanity believes in God, and their image of who God is and what He thinks of us is a large factor in our emotional experiences. If the image of God you created in your mind (from whatever religion you are a part of) results in either an ever-present threat (of judgment, for example) or creates a low level of trust (He isn't good and doesn't notice), that would logically create anxiety. The clearest passage in the Bible on anxiety is Philippians 4:4-8, which states,

> 4 Rejoice in the Lord always. Again I will say, rejoice! 5 Let your gentleness be known to all men. The Lord is at hand. 6 Be anxious for nothing, but in everything by prayer and supplication, with thanksgiving, let your requests be made known to God; 7 and the peace of God, which surpasses all understanding, will guard your hearts and minds through Christ Jesus. 8 Finally, brethren, whatever things are true, whatever things are noble, whatever things are just, whatever things are pure, whatever things are lovely, whatever things are of good report, if there is any virtue and if there is anything praiseworthy—meditate on these things.

Allow me to point out the key points in this passage without exhaustively explaining each part. First, rejoicing is a command where we *choose* to have joy, which is more closely synonymous with peace than happiness. We are to control our emotions, not project negative emotions nor allow them to overflow on others because the Lord is near, which means He cares and is good, and is actively engaged in helping us in the current situation. Because He is good, anxiety is outlawed. Concern is appropriate, anxiety is illegal. The exact same Greek word is used for both "concern" and "anxiety" but one is the right amount of emotional energy produced (concern) which incorporates trust in God as always being good, the other (anxiety) being a result of a lack of trust. This is ultimately from you believing God is not good because He is to blame, or you believe He is not interested or involved. This is a false image of who He is, accusing Him of things He did not do, and saying He is lying because He won't do what He said He would do.

To make sure you don't fall into this, pray and talk to God, and be thankful. Why? Because as you look back, God has always been good and has proven it to everyone. When this current topic is over, and you look back, you will thank Him for being good once again. Pray and ask Him for what you want but thank Him for proving His goodness to you and never failing you. If you do this, peace will overpower your negative emotions without you knowing what's going on behind the scenes. Finally, it is crucial that you figure out what God's opinion on any topic. Whatever the topic, list everything that is true about it, and then how to think and respond in a noble, just, pure, lovely, excellent, and worshipful way. Once you list those sentences, re-read them over and over as you walk through the process until the topic is completed. Anxiety is all about the threat and degree of trust. What I described in Philippians is related to our overall lives and God's engagement with us. Then there are the topics related to having other freewill players involved who have a large say in the outcome that will directly impact you. With those individuals and situations, you may be absolutely right that there is a real threat and absolutely justified in not trusting. Nevertheless, you need to burn all of your energy in the control column through strategy development, controlling what you can control and influencing what you can influence. Countless books can be written on this, but I have already given several techniques in previous chapters that can greatly reduce the threat.

What if the threat is small? Many clients tell me they experience anxiety that is ever-present, and they can't figure out what it is that is causing it. Many clients might know what they are anxious about and know that the threat is small but still results in a full-blown panic attack. I believe the former is from bad past experiences that have convinced their mental models to assume that a threat is always waiting around the corner and at any moment, they are going to have their world rocked again in some way. The latter is the result of the same, but the events were probably of a larger magnitude and have created a short in the fuse of their fight, flight, or freeze mechanism which makes this intense response immediate and frequent. The other very common option is that their experiences that are causing anxiety are very normal, standard, and common, but because of the causes that create inflation (lies, taking things personally, which is related to our IVW, or the carry-over effect from trauma), or a person simply having low resiliency or a low tolerance to stress, or just being weak-minded, creates anxiety and panic that greatly exaggerates the emotion to the threat, even though in reality the threat is minimal.

If the anxiety is ever-present or there is a repeated occurrence of panic attacks, I call that an overstimulated amygdala. The amygdala is the part of our brain in charge of these emotions. When the amygdala is overstimulated, I believe it is way too sensitive to stimuli and needs to be corrected. This can certainly happen through therapy, but I encourage the client to speak to a psychiatrist to see if medication can help. I have no problem with medication because I believe that medication helps stabilize the amygdala to allow therapy to be more effective. I do not believe that anxiety is a permanent state that would result in medication being required for the rest of our lives. I am not a medical doctor, and I am sure there are biological situations where heightened anxiety is a direct result of another biological issue, but those cases are infrequent outliers. No matter what, allow your doctor to be your guide. I do know that every doctor I have ever worked with would adamantly recommend therapy in combination with the medication. If the goal is to have the right type of emotion and the right amount, then you know if the response to the situation you are in truly does require a response of fighting, running for your life, or freezing, then you're definitely not thinking about examining your negative emotions at that point!

My point is that our brains are an incredible creation. When you experience negative emotions, step back and know that the negative energy produced by our brains was designed to be burned off completely. When our ancestors felt fear or anxiety because of the saber-tooth tiger approaching their cave, they would more than likely need that energy to run or fight. If you don't know how to burn the energy completely or where to burn it, then you need to figure out what is being exposed in you first before you do anything (unless you meet a bear out in the woods, then play dead, or run up a tree, etc.). Anxiety is the negative emotion that can be the most present, but the source of it may be hidden. Experiencing ongoing anxiety is bad enough, but it is even more unsettling when a client can't figure out why it is there. Nevertheless, if all biological sourcing has been ruled out, then the fact is you have trained your amygdala to be overstimulated. The brain was created to respond to intense threats through the fight, flight, or freeze response. Knowing this to be true, you need to prove the threat to validate the brain's response. Keep asking yourself, "What is the threat right now?" It may take time to figure it out, especially if it's not a micro, present threat. It may be an overall macro threat, such as a threat to your future quality of life via loss of a job, loss of income, loss of relationships, the state of our world, or the state of our country. As I write this, President Biden just dropped out of the presidential race yesterday. When are you reading this? How did everything turn out? All these things create anxiety in us because there are so many threats out there. However, if it is a macro threat, then you need to return to Philippians 4:4-8 to address it (if you are a Christian). If you aren't, then what are your beliefs about your god, and what does that god say about your future and the future of the world? Who is going to solve this whole thing? If you are an atheist, then please don't tell me you trust in the goodness of humanity! I honestly feel sorry for atheists. The only coping skill is to block it out of your mind and just hope something changes. I'm not a doomsday person, but I also would say if you aren't legitimately concerned about the state of our world, then you are proactively choosing ignorance. I am just going to leave it right there. As Christians, we have an answer to all of this, which is God creating a new heavens and new earth. Humanity just progressively gets worse because it simply doesn't want to submit to God or believes the great lie that God isn't good, so He can't be trusted. That has been the lie since the beginning. That's the answer, but for many of you, the story you tell yourself is enough for you to avoid this altogether and lock it away somewhere in your mind. Please don't.

Now notice what you are feeling right now. Whatever your mental model suggested to you as you read the above either decreased or increased your negative emotions. Your frontal lobe must decide on whether to validate your recent mental model, or you are going to burn energy responding to it by wondering if you are blind to something. You will either continue to write a story that somehow dismisses the above, or you will choose to cry out for insight and understanding and search for it as hidden gold and silver. Yes, I am trying to influence your beliefs, but I am also trying to show you that the anxiety you are feeling is trying to tell you something. You need to ask yourself, ask your soul, what and where is the threat. Again, you may find you are completely at peace, and you have just trained your amygdala to be overstimulated, but you need to do the work to conclude that. We all know that our culture promotes taking anxiety medication long-term or numbing behaviors to distract from doing the inner work. Are you going to turn around and walk through the door or will you continue to stand outside the house of your heart and continue to yell out to anyone who will listen and endlessly talk and lament about what is out of your control? There is an effective answer to responding to what is out of your control, but it is unattainable or unsustainable if you don't first do the hard work of addressing all the rooms in the house of your heart.

Fear vs. Worry

Once the threat is defined, the next logical question would be, "What are you so afraid of? What are you worried about?" These are natural questions, but I want to differentiate between these two negative emotions and then equip you with how to respond to each one. I define fear as the negative emotion produced when something undesirable approaches. The key word of differentiation between fear and worry is *probability.* If the probability of what you are afraid of is high enough, then you have to burn your negative emotional energy, creating a strategy of response to either keep it from happening or minimize the consequences if it does happen. Overall, this is a very natural and healthy process. Worry is also something coming in our direction that we don't want to happen, but the probability of it happening is so low, it can be labeled a lie. For example, when you cry out and say, "Oh my gosh, this will never work out!" or "I'm never going to recover" or "I'll never get a job!" your mental model, again doesn't debate your frontal lobe and just responds with the amount of negative emotional energy that matches the conclusion of your frontal lobe!

Formula Formation: *Emotions don't produce themselves; they come from sentences in our minds. These sentences are opinions, interpretations, conclusions, suggestions, and predictions from the unconscious, subconscious, and conscious mind.*

If these sentences aren't true, then the emotional energy produced will be lower or higher than what is appropriate for the situation. There are certainly many times when we downplay a situation (don't interpret it correctly by stating lies about the impact of the event), which means we won't have the right amount of emotional energy and won't burn that energy in ways that address the reality of the situation. We downplay the impact of our weaknesses, the urgency of a timeline, the need to prepare for a test or presentation, and so on. Only after we suffer the consequences of this consistent downplaying will we begin to change. While this is a common practice for most of us, the opposite problem is far more common, and those who downplay the impact of the situation won't burn the right amount of energy to address the situation; they certainly won't have the energy to pick up and read a book like this. When we have far more negative emotional energy than what the situation needs, it is a result of one of the three causes (lies, IVW, or trauma). I have already addressed how IVW inflates negative emotion. The lies we believe are by far the most common cause of the inflation of negative emotional energy.

These lies come in various forms. We can believe lies about ourselves, about the situation, about the details of the story, about what other people did or said, about God, etc. Earlier, when I was explaining to the tenant that all negative emotions expose something in us, I used the illustration of my immediate processing of my wife, including an evaluation of her character and motives. This is a very common practice all of us have when we are upset with one another. Like the fundament attribution error, we excuse ourselves because we made a poor choice due to our circumstances, while we judge other's character when they make a mistake. We declare our motives to be pure but create lies about others' character and motives. Lies, lies, lies. In Christianity, we know that Satan's number one tool, actually his only tool, is to give us lies, and these lies come in the form of me, He, we. He gives us lies about ourselves, about God's goodness, and/or about our relationship with Him. Lies, lies, lies.

Technique: *The Sentence Dump*

When we are really struggling with something, we have a plethora of sentences running through our minds repeatedly, and it can be maddening. Because emotions don't produce themselves, they come directly from the sentences in our mind, along with the truth that lies inflate our negative emotions, we need to remove the lies to decrease the amount of negative emotional energy. One of the first homework assignments I give to clients is the sentence dump. I tell them to get on their computer and type every sentence that comes to their mind about a current topic. Just allow the mental model to flow freely and dump every sentence, regardless of what it is, into that document, asking them to be careful not to overly evaluate the sentence. Just get in a flow and keep writing. At some point you won't have anything else to write down. Just doing this is cathartic because you get everything out of your mind and can now objectively look at it. I call this "emptying the RAM (random access memory)". Our brains are like computers, and our hard drives (mental models) throw all of these sentences into our RAM. We go back and forth between programs on our computer screen, but our RAM is filled up with all these sentences, slowing down our processing speed and always asking for attention. Once we dump the sentences, they are out of our minds, and immediately, we can feel a sense of clarity.

The next step is to go back and evaluate each sentence. Some of the sentences are just random extreme lies that we can just dismiss and delete, but most of the sentences are more ingrained into our belief systems, and we can't just "delete" them. There is a cognitive technique called "reject by replacing," where the best way to reject lies is by replacing them with truth. Remember, all these sentences are in your mental models. There are formulas in your mental model that produced these sentences, so you need to retrain your mental model very proactively and very intentionally. For example, if your mental model produces the lie, "I'll never get a job!" then you need to replace that lie with a few sentences of truth, even if that truth contains negative sentences. The goal for emotional management is not positivity, it's truth. Once you go through the document and replace all of the lies with truth, then start creating a strategy on how to move forward and respond to your current situation. This is how you respond to fear. There are several things that may cause anxiety, and the threat is a possible outcome that you don't want to happen, but whether it is a fear or worry is 100% contingent on your strategy and its execution. If you have anxiety about an upcoming presentation, an exam next week, or a project at work being completed, then the threat is looking foolish during your presentation, failing the exam, or missing the deadline of the project. Are these fears or worries? Well, if you don't burn energy creating and executing a strategy, then the probability of the threat occurring is high, so it is a legitimate fear. If, however, you burn energy creating and executing an effective strategy, then the probability of it occurring is low and is a worry (a lie). I will now turn to the negative emotion that is chained to the negative emotions of fear and worry: anger.

Anger

There is a key distinction between anger and previous negative emotions. The first four emotions of insecurity, anxiety, fear, and worry are all negative emotions that place us as the underdog in the situation. When we say that we are insecure, anxious, afraid, or worried, we are declaring that there is something more powerful than we are and is having a negative impact on us and is decreasing our overall quality of life. When I show a diagram of the emotional management flow, I place a dotted line between worry and anger. The reason for the dotted line is because the movement from the bottom four emotions to anger is a movement from internal focus to external focus and from negative emotional energy that is *defensive* in nature

FLOW OF INTENSITY		FLOW OF EXPOSURE
	DEPRESSION ANGER -------- WORRY FEAR ANXIETY INSECURITY	DEPRESSION ANGER -------- WORRY FEAR ANXIETY INSECURITY	

to negative emotional energy that is *offensive* in nature. When we are angry, we have decided that we are going to take matters into our own hands and use an intense amount of negative emotional energy to force the situation to change. Anger is a result of unmet expectations, which means something happened we did not expect, or something did not happen that we expected to happen. These unfulfilled expectations result in our personal goals being blocked, and we decide we are going to use anger to remove the obstacles to these goals. For example, someone cuts us off while driving, our boss denies our request for time off, our spouse criticizes us, or our children disobey us. We use anger to correct the obstacle so we can achieve our immediate, tangible goal. When we are angry, we are outside of the house of our heart and burning all our emotional energy on the no-control column and processing, internally or externally, the offense by those who are blocking our goals. Sometimes, we need to immediately burn energy by taking immediate action on our blocked goals, but we all know that an impulse anger response can release far more energy than what is required, which then has its own consequences and causes its own damage. For example, when our children disobey, we get angry because we are disappointed, we scream at them because we are disgusted. When things like this happen and you have time to reflect on it, you need to go back into the house of your heart to figure out what is being exposed in you to have had such a response. Was it one of the causes of the inflation of emotional energy (lies, IVW, or trauma), or was it a result of overall low resiliency or weak-mindedness? To start this process, you need to transition from the tangible goal being blocked to the emotional goal being blocked.

The second goal being blocked, which is what needs to be uncovered, is our emotional goal. All actions that we do are trying to achieve an emotional goal. When you get angry, what emotional goal of yours is being blocked? Sometimes it is difficult to ascertain exactly what emotional goal is being blocked, but it is crucial to figure out what that is to discover why the tangible path being blocked is so important to you. Notice that I didn't say for you to figure out why the blocked tangible goal *is* important, but why is it *so* important. When you screamed at your children, it wasn't simply because they disobeyed you; it was because your emotional goal of feeling like a successful parent was being blocked. You took it personally and believed a lie that your success as a parent was being threatened. Secondly, while it is apparent to determine what bad happens if your tangible goals are blocked, you need to determine what bad happens to *you* if the goal is being blocked. What does it mean to you, what does it say about you? The answers to those questions are revelatory to help us become more emotionally intelligent, as well as address the deeper issues of insecurity and IVW. To assist in the process of uncovering those emotional goals, I encourage women to begin with the emotional goal of security or some form of it, and for men to begin with the emotional goal of significance or some form of it. When you begin there, I believe you then can find synonyms to those words and accurately state not only the tangible goal, but also the emotional goal that is being blocked.

Once you have determined what goals were being blocked, I direct clients to grab those goals and drag them below the dotted line to change the focus from the external to the internal. Even when you determine what goals (tangible and emotional) are being blocked, you need to figure out the degree of response. To do so, realize that in addition to anger being caused by unmet expectations and blocked goals, the degree of anger is always a result of your degree of fear in that moment. Anger ultimately is a result of fear. I have had many push back on that claim, but I always ask them to give one example where this isn't true. We know that we are afraid of not achieving our goals. Fear is at the core of all anger, for every creature. When a cat hunches its back and hisses, a dog bark, or a rattlesnake rattles its coils, it is showing anger as a powerful emotion to achieve the emotional goal of safety, but at its core, it's because it is afraid. Many know the scene from the movie *Batman* after young Bruce fell into the dry well and was overwhelmed by bats. His dad comes to save him and to calm his fears, asks Bruce the question, "Do you know why the bats attacked you, Bruce?" and immediately answers his own question by saying, "It's because they were afraid of you."

When assessing your own fear, ask yourself, "What am I afraid of? What is the worst that can happen if (situation) happened?" Many immediately respond by saying they will feel (insert negative emotion). The negative emotion is not what tangibly happens. It's their emotional response to what tangibly happens. What bad happens or what is the worst that can happen? The answer will be that their tangible goal won't happen (time off, children obey, psycho driver doesn't cut me off, etc.). I then ask the second round of the same question, "What bad happens, or what is the worst that can happen if that happens?" I tell them to keep asking the question until they arrive at the most probable, realistic, and logical result. Normally, when we keep asking that question, we realize that the worst possible thing that can happen (tangibly/physically/relationally) is minor and has a simple solution to it. On the scale of importance, it is normally low (like a one or two), but we responded with a seven or eight. The greatest driving force to applying the third tenant (all negative emotion is exposing something in you) is related to anger. In most cases, our anger is screaming and pointing to our insecurities, our need for others to validate our value and worth, lies we believe about others, or a carryover from past horrible events in our lives. There is great empathy for each other for the hurt we all experience throughout our lives. However, we also all know the truth that the inflated anger in a situation that does not warrant it causes its own damage that may result in those who receive that inflation of anger will now have to recover themselves. What is being exposed in you?

Depression

The final negative emotion in my paradigm is depression. My definition of depression is more practical than medical in nature. If someone is depressed, then the person is still very angry, but they have given up hope that anything will change, but more than that, they have lost grace towards themselves. I do believe that a person who is depressed is still very angry because their goals (tangible and emotional) are still blocked. If they weren't angry, they wouldn't care. Depression comes across as apathy, but that is not the case at all. There is still deep anger and loss related to the blocked emotional goal. The person has burned so much emotional energy trying to achieve their goals that they just get to the point of being burned out, hence the result that they have given up hope that anything is going to change. Hopelessness is a common descriptor of depression. The final piece to the definition of depression is that the person loses grace towards themselves.

I added this piece to my definition after working at the behavioral health hospital. I would always wonder why someone would self-harm when they were depressed. Like anger, depression is above the dotted line, and the focus of the negative emotion is on the environment. Anger is an intense amount of emotional energy burned to change the immediate environment, while depression is a person raising the white flag of surrender to the environment, giving up trying to change it. However, in my work with those precious teenagers, I noticed that after the white flag of surrender was raised, declaring the environment the winner, they would simultaneously declare themselves the loser. After burning all of that energy trying to change the environment to accomplish their goals with no success, they simply conclude that the reason why their environment doesn't change is because of something inherent in them; it's their fault, it's their issue, so they punish themselves in a variety of ways, and in some cases, pass the sentence of death upon their worthlessness and attempt suicide. Not including psychopathic, delusional, or psychotic diagnoses, depression is the most extreme inflation of negative emotions. The lies they believe about themselves, about others, about life, about God, etc. are reinforced in numerous ways, having direct access to their identity, value, and worth. Children who experience emotional, verbal, physical, or sexual abuse, or neglect do not have the emotional or intellectual resources to discern between truth and lies, nor can they arrive at the psychological truth that the authority figures in their lives treating them this way are doing so because of their own emotional, psychological, and moral dysfunction. The negative emotion of depression naturally leads to the topic of trauma.

Conclusion

There are several techniques in this chapter, but the most important is the sentence dump and replacing lies with truth. You need to start exercising self-awareness, noticing the negative emotions and labeling them correctly. What sentences of interpretation, opinion, causation, and prediction are going through your mind that resulted in your negative emotion? As you go day-to-day, find a way to log as many negative emotions as you can, take apart each one, and strategize how you will use the techniques to respond accordingly. This entire process is to help you arrive at the right type and amount of emotion first. Remember, negative emotions are natural, helpful, and necessary. After this, you can select the most RHWR path to achieve your emotional goals.

Chapter 7
The Gift Of Trauma

If IVW is the machine in the basement, then trauma is the dark cellar lurking in the corner that no one wants to open. As you read the title along with the first sentence, I am sure the look on your face was one of confusion and maybe even annoyance or offense. Please continue reading. Hopefully, it will make sense. Before I go deeper, please note that I am in no way trying to lighten or undermine the pain of trauma. Nor am I trying to reframe horrible experiences into positive ones. I have worked a lot with trauma throughout my career and tell clients that while true, diagnosable trauma has specific criteria. Many of us experience trauma when we go through very difficult life experiences. The impact on us is similar, and the process we use to heal from it is similar as well. As I look back, what I thought I knew and truly understood about trauma was elementary prior to my work as a director of a residential treatment center. I created the foundational treatment plan for the therapists. What I oversaw included much of what is shared in this book and used in the course on trauma-informed care for our new employee orientation at the hospital.

As per my usual approach, I always like to ask questions about the common knowledge understanding of certain truths. My first question is asking if trauma happened 10, 20, or 30 years ago, why would it still impact us today? It is understandable if it does, but why does it, especially if the event that caused the trauma only happened one time and nothing like it has happened since? Also, what is it about the trauma experience that completely shocks, paralyzes, and debilitates us? To begin, it is a result of what we call the external locus of control. *Locus* simply means location. This is different than the no-control column described earlier. When it relates to trauma, it means that something outside of me, much more powerful than me, completely unexpected, just came in and rocked my world. The initial shock comes from the concept that I'm going about my merry way, and something outside just abruptly altered my life, and I had no control over it. A powerful example of this relates to our global experience with COVID. Even if I didn't lose someone close to me, something started on the other side of the globe, way over there, eventually made its way around the world and just shut down everyone's quality of life. We had no control over it, were powerless to stop it, and had no choice but to just accept it. That is the very essence of trauma.

The first thing the person does to start processing it is, of course, ask the question, "Why?" Asking why is ubiquitous for every human being who experiences any kind of unfulfilled expectations but is maximized in intensity after a traumatic experience. Again, stepping back, why would people ask the question in the first place. Who are they talking to? When I would ask the class in new employee orientation what they thought the answer was, some would say they were talking to God or the universe. Why would they do that, psychologically? Because I believe they are appealing to something that is greater and has more power than the event or person that caused the trauma. What answer are they looking for? Meaning and purpose. When people ask why it happened, they want to know what possible rationale there could be for this to occur.

There are two kinds of why questions. The first why question is the pre-event why. Why did this happen, what led to this happening, or how did this happen? We want to know the order of events and the reasons behind the decisions made. Ultimately, however, the why question has to do with meaning. I have heard many people say at some point, "I don't know why it happened, but over time, I now understand why it happened." But notice that does not answer the original question, which indicates a desire to know the pre-event rationale for the event to happen in the first place. I will address this more at the end of the chapter.

While we process the answer to that question, there comes a point when we face a fork in the road. I have noticed that every person who has healed from trauma makes a choice to either stay in the column of the external locus of control or move to the column of the internal locus of control by healing or responding accordingly. They quit asking the question why, knowing that they will never have a satisfying answer to the pre-event why and simply state, "It happened. Now I have to figure out how to heal, how to respond to this." Sadly, there are far too many people who stay in the column of giving power to the external locus of control, and they get stuck in their new identity of, "What I lost now defines me." The longer they stay here, they transition from wounded to bitter to entitled. They become bitter because what they lost now becomes a filter through which they view the world. These are the people we describe as continually lamenting, "The world is out to get me!" Eventually, they become entitled because they have a right to justice, and they are going to get it one way or another. This is when we describe certain people by saying of them, "They believe the world owes them something." Somehow many personal conversations land back to the story of their hurt, and they talk about it in detail but want to portray that they have overcome it, but they just "bullet point" their healing experience by saying some form of, "I'm fine, I'm over it" when clearly, they aren't. When clients want to avoid dating people with extreme sensitivity, hyper responses, and constant accusations, I advise them to ask about a past bad relationship and how they healed. If the person details the trauma and lists their healing steps, they are not healed. To those who are here, I ask the same question I have asked myself throughout the years, "Has there ever been anyone who has gone through worse than what I have, and yet came through it successfully healed?" Of course! The best example that can be used is that of Dr. Viktor Frankl, the psychologist who lost his entire family in the Nazi concentration camps, survived, and wrote about his experience in the famous book, *Man's Search for Meaning*. His entire response to his trauma was centered in the journey of his freewill decision to make meaning from his experiences. Obviously, no one can hold a candle to the level of trauma he experienced, but he chose to answer the question *why* for himself.

Thankfully, many have followed in his footsteps and chosen to transition over to the column of internal locus of control and decide to heal. I summarize this process as *in me, through me,* and *for me*. Everyone who heals makes similar statements. I already stated one, "I don't know why it happened, but now I know why it happened." What do they mean? They are making a concluding summary of in me, through me, and for me. *In me,* they say some form of, "I'm stronger now than I've ever been. I wouldn't wish that (the trauma) upon anybody, but I'm stronger now than ever been." There is a stark contrast between those who have and those who have not healed from trauma. Those who have healed are the ones who openly share their story as a story of power, healing, growth, and deep richness. It's the couple who stands in front of the church and talks openly about the affair one of them had, about the porn or alcohol addiction. What do they say? Some form of "As a couple, we are stronger than we have ever been. Of course, we would not wish what we went through upon anyone, but God used it to become stronger than we've ever been." It is the woman who has been sexually assaulted, the child who has been sex trafficked, the alcoholic or drug addict, the spouse to cancer, and it's me, and it's you.

Once we have healed and start to tell our story, we start experiencing that healing is happening *through me*. 2 Corinthians 1:3-4 states, "Blessed be the God and Father of our Lord Jesus Christ, the Father of mercies and God of all comfort, who comforts us in all our tribulation, that we may be able to comfort those who are in any trouble, with the comfort with which we ourselves are comforted by God."[6] While God did not cause the trauma, he absolutely helps us heal from it. His goal is that through our healing, we are able to comfort others and help them heal. When we share our stories, people reach out to us and ask us to connect because they want the same thing. It is an incredibly powerful process. Finally, there is *for me*. This means that our healing ends up blessing us because we have become stronger and more resilient. What do we know about people who have gone through absolute hell yet came out on top of it and better and stronger? We say, "I want that person on my team." I call this the "It" factor. Have you ever said of someone, "They don't get

---

[6] New King James Version®. Copyright © 1982 by Thomas Nelson.

it." or "They totally get it." What is "it"? Those who don't get it, we are not saying it is some level of knowledge about something, but something else. We say they are clueless, that they need to "read the room", or they only see everything through their eyes. But people who truly get it, I think, are the ones who have gone through hell in some way and are stronger because of it. They're stronger, and they're tough-minded, but they are also humble. Why? Because they understand something about themselves. They would probably say, "The only way I was able to become this strong was through that pain, and I would not wish that upon anybody." So, when somebody is around them who doesn't get "it", they don't ridicule that person. Yes, they believe that person is clueless, but they don't demean that person because they realize what it took for them to build this resilience. They become very emotionally intelligent through the process of healing, and they obtain a certain command over life because the annoying things of life don't bother them as much. They are able to keep their cool and respond more objectively to stressors. So, in me, through me, and for me is the process of response in the column of internal locus of control. Here is a diagram of the process:

TRAUMA	
External Locus of Control	**Internal Locus of Control**
Consumed with "Why?"	IN ME
What I lost now defines me	THROUGH ME
Wounded>Bitter>Entitled	FOR ME (RESILIENCY)

How does this process happen? There are many different theories and approaches to healing, but to illustrate, I will use the four-column process, which is a form of Cognitive Behavior Therapy I learned when I was getting my master's degree. In addition to this approach, I have also been trained in Eye Movement Desensitization and Reprocessing (EMDR) therapy, which helps people heal from childhood trauma. I won't go into this therapy in this book other than to say that when a child experiences events they neither have the cognitive or emotional resources for, the trauma becomes an impasse, which simply means the lie they believe about themselves at the moment of the trauma gets stuck. Often, lies many times are centered in some form of they are to blame for the event. Certain therapies like EMDR are needed to "dislodge" the harmful self-interpretations a child created to cope with that trauma. I have used EMDR and other therapy techniques with many clients and it has proven to be very effective.

I will give the diagram of the four-column process now so you can follow along as I walk through it.

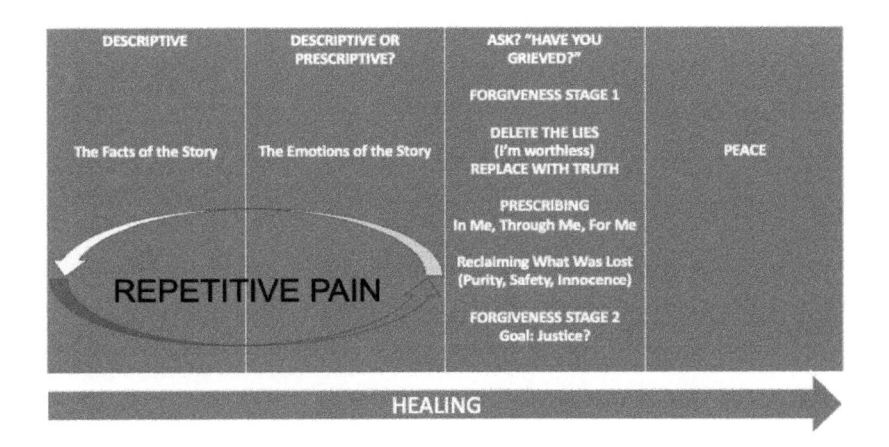

DESCRIPTIVE	DESCRIPTIVE OR PRESCRIPTIVE?	ASK? "HAVE YOU GRIEVED?"	
		FORGIVENESS STAGE 1	
The Facts of the Story	The Emotions of the Story	DELETE THE LIES (I'm worthless) REPLACE WITH TRUTH	PEACE
		PRESCRIBING In Me, Through Me, For Me	
REPETITIVE PAIN		Reclaiming What Was Lost (Purity, Safety, Innocence)	
		FORGIVENESS STAGE 2 Goal: Justice?	

HEALING →

The first step in the process is to have the client open a document on their computer and create four columns. In column one, they just write out the story, just the sequence of events, like a newspaper article. Like the sentence dump technique, something happens psychologically once it's on paper. It may be cathartic, or it may increase the intensity of the story. Considering the potential impact of writing it out, it may take a while to complete it. Column two encompasses the emotions that were and are experienced from the story in column one. When you write the story and the emotions you experienced, it is simply descriptive in nature, meaning it is the story of what happened and what you felt. The emotions also become prescriptive because that is what we carry and experience from that point forward. As time passes, we move on with our lives, but when something in our environment reminds us of the trauma, we go through columns one and two again, process it again, and then we just don't want to think about it anymore. But again, when we drive down the road, see a billboard, see a person who reminds us of the event, we go through columns one and two again, and then the cycle repeats. The problem is it becomes repetitive pain, but worse than that, it increases the frequency because when we experience it again, it creates a new time, date, and place stamp, and every time you experience the same stimuli, it comes back again. Column three is where all the healing work happens. The more work we do in column three, the more our brains automatically link columns one, two, and three, which then automatically leads to column four. Columns two and four are just automatic results of columns one and three.

Now column three, the healing process. The first question to ask is whether the person who experiences the trauma has gone through the grieving process. Some have avoided the hurt and locked it away and the first thing they need to do is grieve and hurt. If they have, then they must enter the gateway to all healing, forgiveness stage one. Forgiveness stage one is simply asking yourself if you have forgiven them. Forgiving someone is sometimes confused with restoring trust and restoring the relationship with that person, but it absolutely is not. Forgiveness is releasing the pursuit to, and authority to, judge, punish, condemn, seek revenge, or bring justice. However, forgiveness is not forgetting, not waiting for an apology, not ceasing to feel pain, not a one-time event, not trusting, not reconciliation, and not losing, it's winning. We need to release the constant vision in our minds of the person who harmed us receiving justice. This is not just a religious process. I have seen countless television shows and movies where the characters motivate one another to forgive, and if they don't, they will be trapped in their pain and be lost to bitterness. Even at the end of some of revenge movies, when the main character is finally face to face with their perpetrator, with the perpetrator's life in their hand, someone is often off to the side yelling, "Don't do it Bob! It won't make you feel any better!" Then the movie ends either with the main character choosing to spare their life, or not. But it becomes obvious either way that the act of revenge doesn't ultimately make them feel any better. So, forgiveness stage one is the gateway to all healing. Without it, the person can't heal.

 This is where I answer the question as to why I believe trauma impacts us so many years later. When I worked with the girls at the RTC, I would tell them that they needed to heal. But I would quickly say, "But to heal, you don't need to process *him* anymore." Logically, they believed in doing so, they would need to process the traumatic event over and over and somehow get to the point where they somehow came to peace with that horrific story. This is absolutely not true. The story is just that, the story. I explained to them that when we experience trauma, there are two things we walk away with that we carry with us that continue to impact us. The first is lies about us, and more important, the impact of what we lost. Even if we were powerless during the event of the trauma, we often tell ourselves the lie that it was somehow our fault or deserved it. When we make any mistakes or fail, the hit our value and worth take is magnified because it reinforces our reasons for the trauma we experienced. If this wasn't bad enough, we lose something in the trauma. What did we lose through those experiences? When I worked with the girls in the RTC, I would ask them this same question (it was amazing how quickly they came up with an answer) they would state they lost their confidence, security, safety, trust, purity, significance, or the feeling they were enough. When one of those elements is lost, it creates a vacuum in us so when we experience situations from that point on where that element is needed, we don't have it to draw from and we suffer for it. We enter situations where we need to draw from our confidence, security, safety, etc., but because we "lost" one of those items, the emotional impact of that situation is inflated. This experience causes negative emotion inflation described throughout the book. I call it the *carryover effect*. When our mental models are in a situation that reminds them of the trauma, they assume the threat is the same and, like a backhoe, scoop the emotional energy from the trauma and dump it on the present circumstance. This is why trauma is still felt so many years later, and if not healed, it will impact us for the rest of our lives. However, this is then the exact process by which we are healed, through reclaiming what we lost. When we reclaim what we lost, it is like the process of healing a broken bone. After a bone heals, it reinforces itself around the break, becoming stronger than before. This is why we say we are stronger after trauma, though we wouldn't wish it on anyone. I will walk through the technique of how to reclaim what we lost at the end of the chapter.

The final step is forgiveness stage two. This is the hardest step, but it is necessary to enter into column four, peace. When I came to this part of the training and walked through it, there were always attendees that I could see were struggling greatly with what to do. If the first stage of forgiveness is releasing the pursuit of justice, the second stage is wrestling with what happens if justice is never served. What does that mean to the healing process? The only way to be completely free is to also release the need or desire for justice. If we can't, then our healing is contingent upon that person receiving justice. We need to completely release even the desire for that person to receive justice. If we can't, we are still linking our emotional health with the no control column, the environment. As Christians, this process of forgiveness is enmeshed with the core of our faith.

The Lord is very clear that if we do not forgive, we will not be forgiven (Matthew 6:15). He also says that whatever measure we use to judge others will be used to measure us (Matthew 7:2). What is justice? It is equal evaluation, equal scales of measurement. If we can't release the desire for them to receive justice, then by definition, we are saying we want justice to be executed on us as well. But then some will say, "Well, that is fine because I would never do what they did to me." That is fair and true. However, we now need to discuss the doctrine of depravity. First, I have noticed that we are all most biased against the sins and weaknesses with which we don't personally struggle. The reverse is also true, meaning there are those who are biased against the sins and weaknesses you struggle with, but they don't. The truth of the doctrine of depravity is that we all are equally depraved in our hearts prior to salvation. This means we all have the *propensity* to sin at the same degree, just in our own "lane" of sin and weakness. The point centers on propensity, not on actual, realized failure, and centers on the fact that we all deserve the justice of the cross, regardless of the quantity or severity of our sins. That is why I believe Christianity to be true, because no one would have imagined the concept that God Himself didn't release the desire for justice. He actually volunteered to take the justice of those who traumatized Him. That is love, and no human being would ever think to create that story because of our own desires for justice for those who have hurt us. Once we complete the final step of releasing our desire for justice and freeing ourselves from our healing being contingent upon it, we finally have peace.

Reclaiming What We Lost

After I ask clients what they felt they lost, I would ask them how they know they lost it to "prove" it to me. I would then ask them what it would look like if they had it back. They understandably have no idea what the answer is to either question. That is where I help them define it. Below is a sample worksheet I use in helping clients reclaim what they lost. If they don't know exactly what it is they lost or feel like they lost several things, we go through the definition of each one to determine which word best describes what they lost. Next, I help them put words to what it feels like when they enter into situations that expose that loss and what it feels like to them. For example, they should have felt secure (or confident, etc.) in that particular situation, but because there is a vacuum, that situation creates the feeling of that loss all over again, even though the situation is completely different. Once someone loses one of those words in a traumatic experience, they have lost it in all situations that resemble certain elements of the original traumatic experience. The goal of having them think through all of these examples is to build self-awareness to prepare themselves for future situations. Next, I then help them create a precise, descriptive picture of what they would be like if they had reclaimed that word (security, safety, trust, etc.). The next piece is to create an acronym of the word and words that would be synonymous or adjacent to the word they are reclaiming, with a short sentence of description that they can lean on and remind themselves of in upcoming situations. Next, I ask the client to be aware of daily situations that test their safety. After that I have them walk through the situation, sit down and reflect and walk through the entire situation again, like a video, moment-by-moment, imagining themselves applying both the description and the words in the acronym to that situation. At every moment, they envision themselves having (security, safety, trust, confidence) in that instant both in what they would think and how they would feel. Through this meditation, they are retraining their mental models and enmeshing that beautiful word they are reclaiming into their hearts and souls. It is a process, sure, but this is the path of healing. I agree that the title of this chapter is incorrect and misleading. Perhaps it should be titled, "The gift that trauma produces." Yes, that is better. Here is an example of a homework sheet I give to clients to reclaim safety:

Reclaiming that which was lost: SAFETY
What is the definition of SAFETY: the condition of being protected from or unlikely to cause danger, risk, or injury.

What does this mean to me currently? What would it look like if I had it? Or how do you prove to yourself that you don't have it?

I dread not knowing what a person's response will be. The fear impacts my entire day. Even though I may truly not know if someone is going to escalate, the degree to which it consumes me is beyond normal. I am controlled by it.

Even if a person escalates verbally, I should be able to have very little emotion because a person verbally escalating literally has no negative effect on me personally. Physically, nothing bad is happening other than their volume on my ears, and if I have control over the situation, I can use skills to actually de-escalate them. So, instead of me feeling I am powerless, I would actually know that I have all of the power.

S *is for strong. My emotional strength is when the environment has very little impact on my emotions.*
A *is for altruistic. When I see anyone (Neil) angry, I will actually have a heart of compassion because the truth is, Neil is afraid. He isn't feeling secure with me, and I want my husband's heart to be secure. He is yelling at me because he is actually afraid.*
F *is for freedom. I know the more I learn these skills, the freer I am. I am free already because I choose to be free from "old Angela". She is scared, I am not. She is insecure, I am not. I am free in the strength in Christ.*
E *is for equal. Neil and I are equal. We equally have struggles. We equally have legitimate complaints, we equally have authority and power in our marriage, we equally love each other deeply, we*

equally want to grow old together. We equally want to grow and have a powerful marriage.
***T** is for tame, teachable, and truthful*
***Y** is for "Yes". My goal in any conversation with Neil is to agree with him as much as it is possible (because his point aligns with truth). I will look for opportunities to say, "Yes, you are right."*

Journal:
How did this play out today? Where did I lack it? What would it look like if I had it? Where did I have it today when previously I wouldn't have (growth)?

The Problem of Evil

As you have noticed throughout this book, people should wrestle with what God thinks of them. More than that, what I find the most troubling is people rejecting God because of the presence of evil in the world. As with many other concepts, I want to be as succinct and specific as possible in order not to lose you in endless theological discourse. Also, the more I discuss intense topics like this, the more I leave the door open for the opportunity for contradictions and inconsistencies. This topic is very difficult and is very emotional for a lot of people.

Here is the problem people have: if God is all-powerful and knows everything, why doesn't He intervene when evil happens? The question is asked in a rhetorical sense because their point is: because God is all-powerful and all-knowing, He should intervene but chooses not to. If God should do something but doesn't do it, that means there is a crack in His character, so He can't be trusted. If He can't be trusted, then that concept is way too troubling to accept, so the best conclusion is to either say you just don't know (agnostic) or that God must not exist (atheist). However, this runs completely contrary to God's goodness. The other major problem with this line of reasoning is the blind confidence in one's own reasoning. Think about it, the person who makes these claims says that they are discerning and intuitive enough to conclude that God should have done something (ethical), but He chose not to do it (unethical). What shocks me is that they didn't conclude that they don't see the whole picture and are missing something, like an explanation, that would make sense. Instead of that, they conclude God is not just. This is why I say that 99% of atheists are emotional atheists. The reason I call them emotional atheists is because something has happened to them, to someone they know, or simply observe what is going on in the world and are angry (or some form of angry) that God is described as good, but then doesn't intervene where they believe He should intervene. I have four absolute truths that I believe address this confusion. These are as follows:

1. God is good. Period.
2. Satan is bad. Period

    If both are absolutes, which they are, then everything that good happens is from God, and everything bad that happens is ultimately traced back to Satan. Instead of beginning your reasoning with "If God is good, then why . . .", begin it with, "Because God is good . . ." in order to find a reason for the problem of evil. It really is that simple, and you need to realize that this is literally the one decision that splits humanity right in two. Satan got Adam and Eve to disobey God by questioning His goodness. This black-and-white distinction was displayed at the cross with the two thieves crucified next to Jesus. One thief questioned His goodness, the other thief began his request with His goodness as a presupposition. At the end of the world, people will cry out against God and choose not to submit to Him because they refused to accept the fact that He is good. Faith is not believing God is powerful, it's believing He is good. If you are agnostic or an atheist, you have faith that God isn't good. Yes, it's faith. If you can't prove it, but make decisions because of it, it's faith.

3. Freewill is a law – God will not override freewill.

When one human being does something terrible to another human being, it is their fault. It's not God's fault. God didn't have anything to do with it. He didn't "allow" it. Those who make this claim imply God said, "Yeah, go ahead and sexually assault them." That is insane. He does not transgress His gift of freewill. Just like you are not culpable for my choices, God is not culpable for yours or theirs.

4. Everything physical is still under laws (our bodies, nature, etc.) so we will get cancer, hurricanes will take people's lives, and so on and so forth.

We were put in charge of the Earth, we decided to abdicate our management to Satan, and he is destroying everything. The Earth is cursed, so the effects from that creates cancer, disease, hurricanes, and floods. God is good. He doesn't "send" these things, Satan does. God is good, Satan is bad.

God will work all things together for the counsel of His will – Ephesians 1:11. This is at a "macro" level, not a "micro" level. Regardless of any freewill choice a person makes (for example choosing to murder a child), God offers to dive in after the event to redeem/restore the negative consequences from the event (Romans 8:28). Remember all four laws above. There are trillions of options and paths that humans will freely choose to take, but none of them can thwart His overall plan. To summarize, He desires to come alongside any human to help restore and redeem, and as believers, our work is to influence everything we can to move it from chaos/disorder to order. Everything we do is to help in that transition. Instead of asking, "Is God good?" flip it to start your processing with, "Because He is good, . . ." He understands our struggles and is empathic when we do struggle, read the Book of Psalms. Once you decide that God is good, and anything that isn't good is not from God, then your pathway moving forward is secure. That one truth is the center of it all. You need to decide on that one thing. If there is any opening in your heart that He isn't, then everything falls apart. The opposite is also true. If God is good and anything bad comes from another source, then your emotional soul is anchored. It is really that simple.

Chapter 8
I³

Why would I wait until the very end to introduce the topic of the title of the book? The process of I³ is a simple, easy-to-memorize system that you can use to incorporate all the concepts of this book. I don't remember when I developed this tool, but it was at least 20 years ago. I have used it in my jobs as a pastor, professor, counselor, coach, and consultant. It became a ubiquitous tool because, everywhere I worked, I saw people living life according to false information, leading to enormous assumptions and narrowness in their thinking that severely lacked critical thinking. Their intense emotion suggests they believe opposing views are guilty of violating these principles and deserve immediate justice, with them eager to execute it. Once you commit this to memory and master the process, you will certainly start to experience the same thing as I have. You will see arguments fall apart before your eyes or will see holes in people's logic so large you'll feel compelled to lunge out to them and yell, "Look out!" to keep them from falling in. Sometimes, you'll stand there with an obvious stunned look on your face and the only words you can muster are, "Bless-your-heart." Let me lay out the paradigm of I³, explain it, and then give multiple examples of how to apply it.

I³: INFORMATION INTERPRETATION INTENSITY

I liken the I³ process to the engineering of the Panama Canal. The Panama Canal was created to greatly shorten the travel time it takes ships to go between the Pacific and Atlantic Oceans. It is located just north of South America in Panama, which is south of Costa Rica. It takes ships eight to ten hours to move through the Panama Canal, but if it wasn't available, it would take approximately 22 days for ships to travel around South America! It is one of the greatest engineering feats that humanity has ever accomplished. It is not like a river where ships just pass through, but a series of locks that fill up and drain to transition the ship from one side to the other. A ship would transition from either ocean into a lock that fills up with water to the height of the next lock, which then fills up with water to the height of the next lock, to the next lock, to the top, which is Gatùn Lake. Then, they do the same process on the way down, with each respective lock emptying its water to the level of the next lock. There are three locks that go up to Gatùn Lake, which is 85 feet above sea level, and three locks that go back down to the ocean. Each lock takes about 20-30 minutes to fill or empty. Use this same engineering concept when using the I³ process.

Information-Interpretation-Intensity
Information

Formula Formation: *It is illegal for me to have any opinion and any emotion until you have all the information.*

Information is simply the story of the event. It is the topic, the data, the facts, and even the assumptions being used to formulate an opinion about what happened and what to do about it. Like the boats in the Panama Canal, you must wait until this first lock is as full as possible before you transition to the second lock, which is your interpretation of the information in the first lock.

He who answers a matter before he hears it, it is folly and shame to him. (Proverbs 18:13)[7]

To answer before listening—that is folly and shame (Proverbs 18:13)[8]

Soon after I re-committed my life to Christ, I fell in love with the book of Proverbs. There is inexhaustible wisdom within that book. Certain verses immediately stood out to me, probably because of the need for me to apply them! Proverbs 18:13 is certainly one. The reason why is that I had so many experiences getting upset about something, only to find out *there was more to the story*, and as soon as I heard the rest of the story, my opinions and emotions would immediately change. I then felt foolish for *jumping to conclusions* and regretted being so consumed with what I heard, and it wasn't even true. When I then read these proverbs and heard God's conclusion that it was folly and shame, I immediately made it a major focus of mine to make sure I applied that in every situation I could. There was a theme I discovered when I struggled the most to apply this wisdom. It was when I *wanted what I heard to be true*. When I heard a story or example that supported my beliefs and opinions, then I readily grabbed a hold of it and used that information myself, only to find out it wasn't true.

The first one to plead his cause seems right, until his neighbor comes and examines him (Proverbs 18:17).[9]

---

[7] The Holy Bible, New King James Version, Copyright © 1982 Thomas Nelson

[8] Holy Bible, New International Version®, NIV® Copyright © 1973, 1978, 1984, 2011 by Biblica, Inc

[9] The Holy Bible, New King James Version, Copyright © 1982 Thomas Nelson

If there was ever a time in human history where this wisdom needs to be applied, it is now. With all our technology and social media which can be either good or evil, there is an addiction to "liking" and "sharing" posts that support your opinion. People are getting hurt and losing their lives from the complete lack of discipline in this area. From online bullying and hating to riots and physical attacks, this is serious. Thankfully, as societies around the globe are starting to suffer the ramifications of this, there is more discernment and more caution being applied by many, but of course, there is no caution whatsoever among many more. We only have control over ourselves and can only influence so many people, but by the grace of God, please try and influence as many as you can to apply this truth. If you ever hear from someone the phrase, "I heard that . . .", then every bell and whistle in your mind should go off to ensure you can't be accused of folly and shame after all the information is revealed.

Walking through this mental model process chronologically, the first thing that happens is the story, however long or short, of he did/she did, he said/she said, or they did/said. Remember that your mental model (DNA, life experiences, choices) is a computer that does not adjudicate what response it gives the frontal lobe (your consciousness) or what comes up on your computer screen. It just uses the information it has gathered since birth and the formulas you have trained it to use throughout your life. The effectiveness of your formulas is a direct product of your logic and reasoning abilities and your critical thinking. Your brain uses a formula to determine how much to engage before forming an opinion, and this formula needs constant adjustment for effectiveness. It's easy and natural to respond emotionally, as that's our instinctive reaction from birth. As our brain develops, we start adding logic and reason to our decision-making processes, but our emotional being isn't so easily tamed. A key concept in Dialectical Behavior Therapy (DBT) is called the Wise Mind Principle. The wise mind is the combination of both the emotional mind and the logical mind. Both are needed in any given scenario. Much of this book has discussed what happens if there is a void of in responding to situations. Emotions are the driving force for us to solve problems and increase our quality of life, but without logic, the consequences of having the wrong amount of emotional energy could be dire. Our mental models offer quick suggestions, but because emotional energy often prioritizes self-interest, we need to pause and let our logical minds contribute. This process demonstrates emotional intelligence skills like impulse control and delay of gratification. By incorporating the formulas from this book, we can train our minds to engage more of our brains in auto-responses. Impulse control is the first EI skill that we need to develop, and it is critical to our experience of negative emotions. Thankfully, it is very easy for us to recognize it when we have negative emotions, so that becomes the red flag for us to pause everything and first assess whether we have all the information. Those who neglect to control their impulses continue to suffer because the environment rules their emotional state.

Whoever has no rule over his own spirit, is like a city broken down, without walls (Proverbs 25:28).[10]

We've all experienced receiving new information after hearing an initial story that completely changed our opinion and how we would have responded. Before we can move on to the next lock, we must investigate the reasoning behind their words or behavior. Have

---

[10] The Holy Bible, New King James Version, Copyright © 1982 Thomas Nelson

you ever been upset with someone who had the right information on the facts of the story, but after they explained why they made the decision they did, it made sense to you, and your opinion changed? Of course, we all have. The information we need to gather before having our own opinion or emotion goes beyond just the external, surface components of the story; it also includes understanding their own mental models and validating before criticizing or judging. There is no way to gather every necessary fact and detail before responding, but we don't have control over that. We do have the control and the responsibility to gather the information we can, do our best to understand the logic and rationale for the decision making, and assume the best of motives and intentions. Once this lock is filled, then the next lock in the canal opens: interpretation.

Fools find no pleasure in understanding but delight in airing their own opinions (Proverbs 18:2).[11]

Interpretation

Formula Formation: *Is there any other way of looking at it?*

Once we have all possible information, then we need to find a way to interrupt the next auto-response of our mental models, our interpretations, opinions, and conclusions of that information. In this step, I simply list three options to help you challenge your models. It is simply negative, neutral, and positive. We don't need any help creating the negative interpretation because that is the automatic response that triggers this process. The first tenet of emotional management is that all emotion is energy. It is either good emotional

---

[11] Holy Bible, New International Version®, NIV® Copyright © 1973, 1978, 1984, 2011 by Biblica, Inc

energy or negative (not bad) emotional energy. Good energy is produced when increasing our quality of life, and the negative energy is produced to solve a problem or react to a "bad" situation. The problem is we often mislabel negative emotions and misjudge the needed emotional energy. To correct this, we must challenge our mental models by ensuring our interpretations are true, replacing lies with more truthful thoughts. Next, we need to practice critical thinking skills by looking at any situation from other angles and other points of view. I suggest neutral and positive interpretations because they are unemotional and logical. The only way to have negative emotions is because our conclusion is that there is a problem to be solved. But what creates the problem in the first place? Remember what created our negative emotions: unmet expectations and blocked goals. Have you ever challenged the legitimacy of your expectations? Have you ever looked back and realized that it was a good thing the paths you tried to take to your emotional goals were blocked? In the last two questions, we just used both a neutral and a positive interpretation of the situation.

Asking yourself if there is any other way of looking at a situation allows you to pause and challenge your immediate conclusion. But how do you discover all of the other ways of interpreting a situation? First, you begin debating yourself and your conclusions. You can put yourself in the place of others and ask, "If someone were to completely disagree with me in the way I'm looking at this, where would they be right?" The goal is to find ways to step out of our subjective selves and into the minds of those with different information and opinions. How would people who have no vested interest in meeting your expectations or achieving your goals view your situation? Where would they be right? What about those who disagree with your expectations and the ways you choose to meet your emotional goals? Where would they be right? We're not looking to eradicate your opinions, interpretations, or judgments, we want to obtain *all* the opinions, interpretations, and judgments that are true so we can know how to respond effectively to any situation. Remember, we all have blind spots, so proactively seek insights from others who have more accurate and effective mental models. But don't be discouraged—they need yours too.

Without consultation, plans are frustrated, but with many counselors they succeed (Proverbs 15:22).[12]

I also will reach back and pull in the concepts of rational, healthy, wise, and right (RHWR). Another way to both debate our original interpretations, as well as add new ways of thinking about our situation is to use the RHWR paradigm. Remember, we are all accountable for this paradigm, but we can also appeal to it. We hold ourselves accountable to it by asking, "Are any of my opinion's irrational? Are they unhealthy? Unwise? Or just plain wrong?" Additionally, we can appeal to RHWR after we have filtered all our opinions through this paradigm, and once an opinion passes the test, we can hold on to it with all of our might and allow it to guide our responses. I use the RHWR grid a lot in my marriage counseling. As you might imagine, both the I³ and the RHWR process are very needed in marriages! Or maybe you don't need to imagine this at all because you are married, and you get it. Among all of the reasons couples seek marriage counseling, I cannot think of one time when a couple reached

---

[12] New American Standard Bible, Copyright © 1960, 1971, 1977, 1995, 2020 by The Lockman Foundation, La Habra, Calif.

out to me, and communication wasn't on their list of reasons for seeking therapy.

What area do the principles in this book better apply than within the context of marriage? If you aren't married, then it is either in your dating or family relationships. You feel the most exposed with those to whom you are closest. Why? Probably because your value and worth are still tied to your spouse pursuing and validating you. Or it may be that you feel your spouse is regularly blocking your emotional goals of significance or security. There are multiple reasons! Every couple has topics they need to discuss and work through, but that is not the problem. The problem arises when we attempt to discuss those topics. Our negative emotional energy gets inflated, and we hurt each other in *how* we talk (or yell) to one another, causing damage to the relationship. We now must have another conversation to recover from how we hurt each other before we can get back to working through the original, legitimate topic that started this whole mess. But alas, many never get there because their "how" is so bad that they cannot get through the "what." There are many communication techniques I give to couples to help them become more effective in their communication. I have recorded a video and have a slide deck you can download to go over with one another. Just got to my website (www.becomingmore.com), then go to "Resources and Forms" and scroll to the bottom of the page.

One of the problem-solving techniques I give to couples walks them through how to use the RHWR grid to solve problems. Let's break down an argument. Whenever two people argue, there are many points of agreement and many points of disagreement. However, what I have found is after all the monologuing, each person only has one main point. It can also be said that each person has just one main goal they want to achieve throughout the discussion. Where we go awry are all the sentences, opinions, supporting evidence, and links to other related issues *that orbit around the main point*. In those elements exist all the non-RHWR comments, and why we go off on tangents and never solve the original problem.

I advise couples to go through this exercise when they come back together after an argument to help them recover from the hurt and start over. To hold ourselves accountable to the grid, we should use the actual words in our sentences to one another. "It is/is not rational that I/you . . . It is/is not healthy when I/you . . . It is/is not wise that I/you . . . It is/is not right that I/you . . ." If you can go through this exercise without firing up the trigger engines again, then do it because it can be very healthy and powerful. However, if you don't, it is okay. Save it to the end after you both agree on a solution, and then come back and walk through the repair process.

During the time you are both separate, trying to cool down from the argument, spend that time evaluating the statements of your spouse that *are* RHWR, and the statements you made that were *not* RHWR to keep yourself out of pride, burning all your energy on just the opposite. After you complete this, push yourself to sift through all of your spouse's statements to uncover their main point. What is their main point? Is their main point RHWR? Then do the same for you. What is my main point? Is my main point of the argument RHWR? 99% of the time, these main points will pass the RHWR test. If we say, "Look, my main point is . . ." we state our point in a succinct, accurate, simple way, and when we do that, it is easy to see it is RHWR. When you come back together, simply clarify one another's main points until you both agree that you understand each other. You will see that each point transforms into your main goal when you start discussing solutions. After this, skip over all those statements you stated that orbit around your main point, and start discussing the solution. What is the most RHWR response/solution moving forward that achieves both of your goals (main points)?

The last point I want to make for this section is to remind you of what I stated in the first chapter. Finding other ways to look at a situation takes a lot of humility and work, but this is exactly what the Lord meant when He told us to cry aloud for knowledge, insight, wisdom, and understanding. Search for it like we would hidden treasure, *for then we would understand the fear of the Lord*. The fear of the Lord can mean very different things. For those who see Him as good, the fear of the Lord is centered in a humble understanding that there is so much we do not see or understand, but He does. We naturally think that when we fear something, we run from it, but because He is good, we run *to* Him. We fear Him because we are blind and need His insight for all things, which is humility. Those who do not see Him as good run from Him because they believe they already have the intelligence and wisdom to declare that He isn't good and fear Him because they assume He will only hurt them.

Intensity

You can tell that filling the second lock is an intense but powerful process. Once you've identified true and logical opinions across the negative, neutral, and positive spectrum that pass the RHWR test, you'll naturally have the right emotional energy to make the most effective decision. However, even with this success, you'll likely need to do further internal work to address what was revealed during the process. Each situation we encounter should stand alone so as not to drag in other topics related to the current situation or add too much emotional energy from the deeper areas of our souls. The I^3 process allows you to do that. Doing the deeper work of understanding what's exposed in you is crucial to prevent inflated emotional energy in future situations. This process makes you more resilient and tough-minded, reflecting your strength, reclaiming what was lost from past trauma, and solidifying your core identity, value, and worth.

You can't impart what you don't possess. As I wrote this book, there was a great peace and confidence I felt, knowing that I have fully saturated my heart with all these principles, truths, and techniques. Actually, the entirety of these principles, truths, and techniques were the product of my own exposure, my own insecurities, my own pain, and my own wrestling with what I knew to be true and holding tightly to it as it pulled me through the most powerful periods of my life. I thank God for being so good, Jesus for being my First Love and Fiancé, and the Holy Spirit for allowing me to taste and experience His signs, wonders, and miracles. I also thank my mentors, my friends, my seven kids and their spouses, and my wife, who is the absolute proof of the grace of God in my life.

The Power of I^3:
What is the most emotionally intelligent RESPONSE?

INFORMATION (Data)
- Do I have all of the information?
- *It is illegal to have any opinion or any emotion until I have all of the information.*

INTERPRETATION (-   N   +)
- Is there any other way of looking at it?
- *Wisdom means interpreting the situation through all truths.*

INTENSITY (1-----------------10)
- How much emotional energy is needed to respond to the situation?
- *What is being exposed in me?*

Milton Keynes UK
Ingram Content Group UK Ltd.
UKHW040739101124
2717UKWH00001B/2

9 781666 410594